PRESTON PUBS

STEPHEN R. HALLIWELL

AMBERLEY

The Bull & Royal Hotel in Church Street.

First published 2014

Amberley Publishing
The Hill, Stroud
Gloucestershire, GL5 4EP

www.amberley-books.com

Copyright © Stephen R. Halliwell, 2014

The right of Stephen R. Halliwell to be identified
as the Author of this work has been asserted in
accordance with the Copyrights, Designs and
Patents Act 1988.

ISBN 978 1 4456 3858 4 (print)
ISBN 978 1 4456 3875 1 (ebook)

British Library Cataloguing in Publication Data.
A catalogue record for this book is available from
the British Library.

Typesetting by Amberley Publishing.
Printed in the UK.

Introduction

The prospect of researching the old inns and taverns of one's place of birth would, at first glance, seem to be something approaching a dream endeavour, and yet the reality came by a rather circuitous route – particularly for someone who has been alcohol-free for seven or eight years.

The circuitous route to which I refer begins with me being a lifelong naturalist, and the fact that when I was in my early teens, a book about the birds of the British Isles introduced me to the St Kilda wren, a bird that is endemic to a small island called St Kilda in the North Atlantic. The closest I got to establishing the position of the island was to find it in a supplementary box in the top left-hand corner of a Bartholomew's half an inch to the mile map of Western Scotland. I got no further, and forty years of working life slipped by.

Then, in my late fifties, an age by which I had allowed a passion for the Outer Hebrides to develop, I once again heard about the mythical island of St Kilda, so I determined to visit it. It's not an easy place to get to, but there are specialist tour operators on the west coast of Scotland and Harris in the Outer Hebrides that will transport visitors. I have been four times, and on each occasion I travelled with Northern Light Cruising Tours out of Oban. Excellent!

However, my visits to St Kilda, almost from the first moment I set foot on the island, created an interest in the social history of the place – an interest that became almost an obsession, reading all the available literature that had been published.

It reached a point where I started to ask myself why I'd never been interested in the social history of the place I've spent the first sixty-nine years of my life. The thought became stronger and more powerful, until a point was reached where I made a decision to do something about it. I made a list of the things that I thought were worthy of research, and with which I would have an equally enthusiastic approach. From memory, my list included the life and times of Preston's Theatre Royal, which was built for the 1802 Preston Guild Festivities; the tidal length of the River Ribble and its history; the history of the Preston Borough Police Force, one of the earliest in the country; and finally, the one that I selected, the history of Preston's hotels, inns, taverns and beerhouses.

There seems to have been nothing attempted in terms of recording the history of perhaps one of our most divisive creations – the alehouse and its fellows. They have been perhaps exaggerated in Preston by the work of Joseph Livesey and his Temperance Movement, a movement that was intensified when he declared that total abstinence was their ultimate objective.

Despite Livesey and his associates pressuring the magistrates of the day to refuse new licences, and where appropriate remove existing licences, I have still been able to identify 803 such establishments before the outbreak of the First World War. For the purpose of this book, I have not made any distinction between those that were just beerhouses and those that were able to also sell wine and spirits, and there are also a number of instances where one house has had two or more names. In many instances it is impossible to be absolutely sure of a continuation of a property under a different name, and so I have assumed them to be different. Many beerhouses, for instance, were merely an adapted front room of an otherwise ordinary terraced cottage.

In 2012, as a consequence of the research I had completed, I created a website in the form of a blog. Blogs are a wonderful way to let people know what you know, and they also give others the opportunity to add to that knowledge. That is exactly what has happened. I have included an image of a public house where they are available, a list of the landlords and landladies, a transcript of the censuses where appropriate, and copies of anecdotal material that has been gleaned from mainly nineteenth-century newspapers.

The site has attracted attention from the four corners of the world, particularly family historians who have been looking for their relatives, with many finding them, unexpectedly running a hostelry.

I am not one of the local historians who keeps his knowledge close to his chest; I really don't see the point, but I'm sure they have their reasons. My belief is that knowledge is there to be shared, and that by working together either as a group or with individuals, anomalies that certainly exist can be addressed. Information that I have been able to pass on has been repaid with information that could only come from within the family.

I have included a motto in my blog that I will repeat here. As far as I am aware it is my own creation, but I could have picked it up anywhere along life's corridors:

Sowing a single seed on this website could lead to an abundant harvest!

I sow one again here, and would be delighted to hear from anyone who can add to my knowledge.

Chapter One

The Inner Circle

In the first chapter of this book we will look at the hotels, inns, taverns and beerhouses that have existed a mere 500 feet or so from the Old Town Hall, on whose foundations Crystal House currently stands. In the year 1800, much of Preston's activity, both economic and social, will have occurred within that radius, and with almost all of it occurring within the bounds set for Chapter Two.

The radius of 500 feet will take us along to a point opposite The Minster on Church Street and to a point a little beyond Guildhall Street on Fishergate. After crossing the ancient market place and entering Friargate, we won't progress even half the distance to Orchard Street before reaching the edge of our circle. In a southerly direction, the same circle's edge will be reached before meeting the bottom of Glovers Court. Unsurprisingly, the establishments that have replaced the inns and taverns of yesteryear are still condensed in the same area, but more of them another time.

As a market town of some importance, the greatest activity took place in and around the market place, where separate areas were designated to purveyors of cheese, fish, butter, and so on. The attendant gatherings of customers of the market traders, as well as other retailers in the vicinity, presented many opportunities to cater for the needs of all those individuals, as well as the stabling and welfare needs of the many horses that would have carried them there.

Throughout the nineteenth century, the market place was almost entirely enclosed by buildings. During the final fifteen years of the century, during improvement work by the Corporation, the northern and eastern sides of the square were demolished to make room for the grand Harris Museum and Art Gallery, and other buildings. The area on the east side of the square, in particular, was intersected by narrow alleyways with even narrower entrances, all of which ran towards the Shambles, now known as Lancaster Road, with some of them opening out onto that thoroughfare.

The principal alleyways, from north to south, were Gin Bow Entry, the Strait Shambles, Blue Anchor Yard, and Clayton's Court or Yard. On the northern side of market place, the narrow New Street – barely 20 yards in length – contained three inns next door to one another. The Old Shambles and Cheapside afforded exits on to Church Street and Fishergate respectively at points either side of the Town Hall, with

The city centre, an area whose structure has change remarkably little over the last 200 years.

KEY
1. George Inn
2. Virgins Inn
3. Golden Ball Inn
4. White Bull Inn
5. Swan or White Swan Inn
6. Cross Keys Inn
7. Wheatsheaf Inn
8. Ram's Head Inn
9. White Hart Inn
10. Shoulder of Mutton
11. Golden Lion
12. White Horse Hotel
13. Anchor Inn
14. Mitre Inn, Market Place
15. Shakespeare Tavern
16. Swan-with-two-necks
17. (Original) Golden Cross Hotel
18. Blue Anchor Inn
19. Haymarket Tavern
20. Red Lion Hotel
21. (Original) Stanley Arms
22. Old Red Lion
23. Crown Hotel (incorporating the Old Red Lion after 1827)
24. King's Arms Hotel
25. Grey Horse (Yates)
26. Bull & Royal Hotel
27. Eagle & Child
28. Turk's Head Tavern
29. Old Cock Inn
30. Garth's Arms
31. Humphrey's Clock
32. Sun Inn
33. Golden Ball
34. Old Legs of Man
35. Wellington Inn
36. Mitre Inn, Fishergate
37. Shelley Arms Hotel
38. Castle Inn
39. Golden Lyon
40. Grey Horse & Seven Stars
41. Borough Tavern
42. New Legs of Man
43. Black Bull, Cheapside

Friargate leaving the square in its north-west corner. Where Friargate meets the square there were two small streets or alleyways, one on either side, with Anchor Court to the west and Anchor Weind to the east.

So, let's make a start and have a closer look at a select group of these premises, bearing in mind that there are no existing images for many of them. There will be a concentration on those premises for which there is an image, and for those for which there isn't, I'll be as descriptive as I am able in order to bring them back to life for my readers. Although the inns and taverns will be dealt with in alphabetical order in each chapter, an exception has been made in this chapter. I think it will make it easier to understand if the eight premises that were lost to provide the ground for the construction of the Harris Museum, and so after the initial Anchor Inn in Anchor Court will be described in succession.

ANCHOR INN, Anchor Court (1678–1807)

Despite there being no images of this inn, it was repeatedly referred to in the diaries

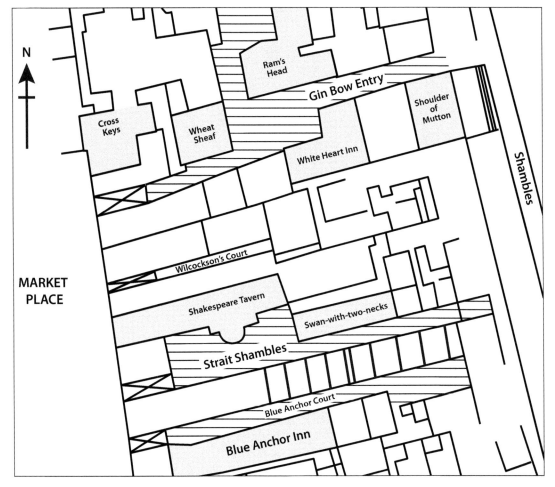

A plan of the area now occupied predominantly by the Harris Museum and Art Gallery.

The Blue Anchor Inn

of both Col. Rawsthorne and Bellingham from around 1683, and was clearly a place of retreat for the gentry, it has also been referred to as the 'Golden Anchor'. Anchor was a word with religious connotations, but in the Great Court Leet dated 26 April 1699, there was a mention of it as 'The Anker', and on another occasion it was referred to as the 'Three Tuns'. An anker was a pre-metric European measure of liquid, particularly in Holland, a country with which Preston had a number of important trade connections at the time. A tun was also a measure for liquids. The derivation of the name is, therefore, open to debate. Its precise position in Anchor Court is also the subject of debate to this day.

BLUE ANCHOR INN, Blue Anchor Court (1790–1883)

The court was entered by means of a narrow, covered passageway, over which was displayed an anchor to announce its presence within. At the point where the court widened, on the right-hand side, stood the inn where, it is said, Joseph Livesey, of total abstinence notoriety, drank his last pint of ale while taking a break from his market cheese stall.

In its early days, it was the resort of many of Preston's leading individuals, and they would meet in a room that earned the name 'House of Lords'. It was in this same room that John Horrocks, when he was town bailiff in 1794/95, was requested to stand for the borough in Parliament. It can be seen in the photograph that above one anchor, there is another less obvious one, possibly indented or embossed on the wall. There remain discussions as to whether the name is from this origin, or the ones mentioned previously.

The Blue Anchor had the best recorded history of all those inns and taverns that formed part of the town that comprised a complex of small businesses in a series of narrow alleyways between the market place and the Shambles, now Lancaster Road.

CROSS KEYS INN, Market Place (c. 1684–1894)

The Cross Keys stood in the north-east corner of the market place, close to the narrow entrance of the curiously named Gin Bow Entry. Although I have a date stretching back to about 1684 for it, other records between that date and the early 1800s are scant. There were up to ten inns and taverns that were sacrificed to clear the way for the erection of the marvellous Harris Museum and Art Gallery, and the only reason for such a late closing date is that the Corporation, who had compulsorily purchased all the properties involved, had moved the licence to an adjacent property and continued trading under the same sign.

A single shop, over which the first floor of the Cross Keys ran, divided the Cross Keys from the covered alleyway to Gin Bow Entry – a narrow entry, but not as narrow as the others that ran parallel to it. It was also the only one that required the pedestrian to climb steps to access it. For the undoubted convenience of passersby, there was a gaslight at its entrance. Preston was the first place outside London to have street lighting, thanks to the work of the Revd Joseph 'Daddy' Dunn, who, with his partner, Isaac Wilcockson, the proprietor of the *Preston Chronicle*, whose name is memorialised in the narrow court next to Gin Bow Entry, introduced piped gas to the town and other parts of Lancashire. As we emerge from the far end of the short, covered entrance to Gin Bow, we are met on the left of the alley by the Wheatsheaf Inn.

WHEATSHEAF INN, Gin Bow Entry (1804–81)

The Wheatsheaf undoubtedly precedes the date shown because 1804 was the year that the wife of the landlord, Thomas Rigby, died, but no other documented evidence exists. Access to Gin Bow for those other than pedestrians was from what is now Lancaster Road, including access to the stables attached to this inn. How many there were isn't known, but in 1842, as a result of carelessness by the ostler employed there, two horses were burned to death, with the ostler absconding.

In a notorious case in 1870, the licence of the Wheatsheaf was objected to by the police because of the behaviour of landlord John Parsons' wife. It was said at the Brewster Sessions of that year that 'she had studied the art of fisticuffing', and that 'one night she had given a police constable and a sergeant a practical illustration of her hitting powers'. The police had been in the process of making a routine visit to her house 'when she commenced with her fists, and gave the sergeant a good thrashing'.

Having initially objected to the renewal, the police then told the court that, when sober, Mrs Parsons was a good landlady and the licence was granted. Continuing our walk through the Gin Bow, the next inn on our left is the Ram's Head Inn.

RAM'S HEAD INN, Gin Bow Entry (1750–1881)

It has been said that sheep are very rarely depicted on inn signs in the UK, but perhaps with the lamb being closely linked to our city's crest, Preston is an exception to the general rule. Rams and their heads are more frequently seen, yet are far from common. Our earliest knowledge of this inn was when Michael Emmett was the landlord. He was a member of a well-respected family who were involved with the building trade. In fact, they rebuilt the town hall in 1782. Michael had seven sons, the second eldest of whom, also called Michael, became one of the earliest Methodist ministers in Preston, marrying the daughter of the Methodist Crane family. In 1780, she entertained the Venerable John Wesley on one of his visits through Lancashire. The eldest son, John, after several years in exile in Woodplumpton, designed the obelisk that stands at the southern end of the market place.

While at the Ram's Head, Michael Emmett made his fortune, and when he died he left £500 to each of his eleven children. When he retired, Emmett handed the inn over to James Howard. Howard's reputation as a purveyor of strong ale grew rapidly, and in the Election Expense Records of 1796, the inn was referred to by its colloquial name of 'Ram Jams'. It was known as 'Old Ram Jams' because the ale he supplied was so strong that it had been said that 'he rams 'em in on one side, and jams 'em in on t'other'. Coincidentally, Howard also had a son called John, who was a devout Methodist and one of the founders of Lune Street Methodist church.

Across the entry from 'Ram Jams' we see its close neighbour, the White Hart Inn.

WHITE HART INN, Gin Bow Entry (1805–82)

The third tavern with an address in Gin Bow Entry is the White Hart. When it was sold in 1806 by the Earl of Derby to James Forshaw, the sitting tenant, it was described as having stables and a brewhouse, so the prospects of it existing to a date considerably previous to that shown are great.

There have been several references to it being a market tavern, set up to meet the needs of those visiting the town for business purposes. In the auction notice of May 1807 it was described as a 'well-accustomed Inn or Public-house, with the stable and premises adjoining', with another lot being described as 'a good stable for eight horses, plus a room over it used as a wareroom'. The last lot was in Ward's End, immediately across the Shambles from Gin Bow Entry.

Although many of our town centre inns and taverns appear to be cramped together – and there are no finer examples than those in Gin Bow Entry – they seem to have had sufficient space inside them to offer extensive catering facilities. There's little doubt that most, if not all, were in purposeful first-floor rooms that could be used for a multitude of events. In 1843, for instance, the 'Forester's Grove' Court of the Ancient Order of Foresters celebrated their anniversary at the White Hart, when over 100 members and friends 'sat down to a sumptuous supper'. The meal was followed by songs and glees, and a lecture by Mr Corless, surgeon, entitled 'Sleep, Somnambulism, and Digestion'. It was reported that the meeting was 'kept up with spirit until the clock struck the hour of twelve o'clock'. As we leave the open-ended Gin Bow Entry, we meet, on our right-hand side, the Shoulder of Mutton.

SHOULDER OF MUTTON, Shambles (pre-1785–1881)

The Shoulder of Mutton had been standing in the butcher-dominated Shambles since

The Shoulder of Mutton in the Shambles.

at least 1785, and probably much earlier. It survived until 1881 when it became one of the properties to be demolished under a compulsory purchase order. The inn stood at the corner of Gin Bow Entry, which took the course of the current Harris Street from the market place. On the opposite side of the Shambles stood the narrow thoroughfare known as Ward's End (known colloquially as 'World's End'), which provided access to St John's Street, later renamed Tithebarn Street and Lord's Walk.

Since the construction of the Guild Hall, Ward's End has been resited 20 yards to the south, and adjacent to the Stanley Arms Hotel. The Shambles followed the route now known as Lancaster Road, and during the time that most of the retail properties were those of butchers, animals of all types were slaughtered in the street and prepared for sale. Having entered the Shambles and walked south a few steps, we meet the covered entry to the Strait Shambles, which we enter and walk back towards the market place. Having walked between two rows of butchers' stalls, the passage opens out to a small courtyard where two taverns stand. Immediately to our right is the Swan-with-two-necks.

SWAN-WITH-TWO-NECKS, Strait Shambles (1803–81)

There's no doubt that the existence of this inn precedes the date shown. The first indication I have was when Mrs Ann Sumner was the landlady. In that year she appears in the records of the court leet, when she was to be fined 40 shillings if she did not address a problem with a well at the entrance to the Strait Shambles, and for which she was to have repaired within one week. It would have been unusual for a woman to take an inn such as this one on her own, and it is assumed that her husband had preceded her as the landlord.

From a very early date the inn was connected with a butcher's shop, and there is evidence that more than one landlord here was also a butcher by trade. Indeed, there is a lot of anecdotal evidence to show that the Swan-with-two-necks tavern was a meeting place of choice for the scores of butchers who traded in the Shambles area.

Although it is well documented that the concert hall has its roots in the public house, there were many that offered a rather crude form of the genre in the early days. This was one such establishment when, in 1840, the police court was told that the room used as such was often a backdrop for disorderly scenes, and the magistrates recommended to the police that this and others like it should be carefully watched, 'for there can be no doubt that they are the most fruitful tanneries of crime and dissipation of every description that can be inflicted on any community'.

SHAKESPEARE TAVERN, Strait Shambles (1818–71)

Barely half a dozen strides separated the front doors of this tavern and the previous one. While the first date for this one is inaccurate, there is very little evidence to tell us by how much. There is evidence that part of the premises were apart of the ancient Mitre Tavern that faced the market place until around 1768, when the licence and the name were transferred to a property on the south side of Fishergate. The replacement Mitre Inn was described as 'well-established' by 1790.

In 1715, the original Mitre Inn had featured in the surrenders of 1715, when the commoners in the troops surrendered their arms in the market place while the officers were allowed to lay theirs down in the inn itself. The covered entrance to the Strait Shambles was called 'Mitre Court'.

There are several examples of pedestrianism being held from the Shakespeare. In 1832, Robert Skipper, a man of pedestrian notoriety, walked 50 miles a day for twelve successive days, excluding Sunday. He began in Lancaster and walked to the Shakespeare Tavern, where he would have his breakfast before making the return journey. Although there is no record, this sort of sporting endeavour was usually accompanied by betting on the outcome – though from the records I have, Skipper himself claimed that the only reward for his labour were from contributions from a generous public.

Although both of the inns in this passageway must have benefited from the proximity of the market place, this, unlike the Swan-with-two-necks, offered to 'accommodate gentlemen, on the shortest notice, with chops, steaks, or dinners'. It is interesting to note that the landlord offering this service is the same James Leigh who had been fined for fighting when he was at the Swan-with-two-necks three months earlier.

The Shakespeare Tavern ceased to trade in 1871, and for the last ten years of its existence it was a joiner's workshop occupied by a man called Chippendale.

BOAR'S HEAD INN, Friargate (c. 1732–1983)

The first inn on the west of Friargate was the ancient White Horse Inn, and a few doors further down stood this subject. There was another Boar's Head in this thoroughfare, further north and on the east side of Friargate Brow, shown on

The Boar's Head Inn.

Cuerden's map of 1684, and so references to this inn from that era have always presented an identification problem. The 1732 date is from the court leet records, but there is no clue given to identify it with certainty.

Its proximity to the market place always ensured full participation in the economy, including the many visits to Preston of travelling circuses and menageries. In November 1818, there was an advertisement announcing that during the approaching fair, there would be an appearance at the Boar's Head of 'the largest alligator ever landed alive in England, being upwards of nine feet long'. It went on to explain 'the enormous creature is very ferocious, but that it is so properly secured that the most timid lady may approach him without fear or danger'.

BOROUGH TAVERN, Fishergate (1852–1917)

Further reminders of the old burgage system can be seen with this pair of neighbouring taverns set on the north side of Fishergate, directly opposite Cannon Street. The Borough Tavern was bounded on the west by Walton's Yard, and on the east Sumner's Yard, which separated it from the Grey Horse and Seven Stars Inn. The Borough Tavern lay behind and above the Palatine Rubber Company shop premises, and was announced not only by its sign, but also a large, embossed borough lamb, together with the familiar P. P. of 'Proud Preston', or more accurately 'Princeps Pacis', Prince of Peace. The sign is now in the Harris Museum.

The Borough Tavern. *Inset:* The inn sign.

It is thought that this name may have been a progression from the 'Holy Lamb', for this is what the place was called in 1684, and presumably had a lamb in its signage. There is, however, a huge gap between that and any evidence of its successor, for the earliest mention I have for the borough is 1852, when it was operating as a tavern and commercial hotel.

After the First World War, the property was bought by the forerunner of the *Lancashire Evening Post*, as was the Grey Horse and Seven Stars, and their premises were a familiar city centre sight for well over fifty years.

BULL AND ROYAL HOTEL (formerly THE WHITE BULL),
Church Street (1670–present)

There is a school of thought that suggests that this hotel didn't have its origins in the White Bull that stood on the site before it, but I feel that the weight of evidence is in its favour. This Grade II-listed building was one of the major coaching inns in Preston, and has been linked with many of the memorable and sometimes turbulent events in the city. It is known that the 'White Bull' was used as judges' lodgings when magistrates were travelling to or from the Lancaster Assizes. One such lodger was the notorious Judge Jeffreys, Lord Chief Justice of England in 1684.

Aristocratic users of the hotel included the 4th and 5th Dukes of Hamilton, and Bonnie Prince Charlie held council here in 1745 on his journey south. In 1773, Lord Stanley, 12th Earl of Derby, bought the hotel, and although several of the Stanley family were later to become politicians, the 12th Earl was totally disinterested in politics, caring more about his social life and sporting interests. In 1774, the Earl also

The Bull & Royal Hotel.

bought the property neighbouring the White Bull. He rebuilt the front of the property and constructed what became known as the 'Derby Assembly Room', or the 'Adam Room' because of its Adam-style decor. It is this magnificent room that has earned it the protection of English Heritage's Grade II-listed status. In 1913, King George and Queen Mary dined in this room on a visit to Preston.

Daniel Defoe is also likely to have used this hotel on his visit to Preston, and Charles Dickens, in 1856, stayed here while he assessed the poverty and suffering of the people due to the millworkers' lockout – his subsequent book *Hard Times* is believed to be based on Preston, with Dickens referring to it as 'Coketown'. On the occasion of one of radical Henry 'Orator' Hunt's visits to the hotel, his horse Bob died in the stables and was buried in a garden at the rear of one of his backer's houses in High Street. Seven or eight years later, Bob's bones were exhumed, and in their various portions were a prized piece of memorabilia among Hunt's many supporters.

Today, the Bull and Royal Hotel no longer offers accommodation, but continues to present a selection of entertainment, including live music.

CASTLE HOTEL, Market Place (1623–1905)

This important old coaching house on the west side of the ancient market place was erected in 1623, and demolished in the 1930s. It is believed that in its early days it was the town house of the Rawsthorne family of Hutton. That family still owned it in the 1930s when it was sold to the proprietors of the *Preston Guardian*, the third licensed premises to be acquired by them, along with the Borough Tavern and the Grey Horse and Seven Stars (the Fishergate twins). The Castle Hotel had a considerable depth back from the market place, and extended well beyond the rears of the two Fishergate public houses.

During the nineteenth century it was esteemed by the county gentry, and it was not unusual for up to thirty conveyances to be accommodated on a daily basis. The bay windows, one of which had a bunch of gilded grapes hanging above it, and the large coach entrance were constant features throughout its life. When it was demolished it was said that 'something picturesque' had disappeared from the square.

In 1826, William 'Gridiron' Cobbett, the great radical, addressed a crowd from one of the windows when he was a parliamentary candidate for Preston. He did the same thing again in 1830, while supporting Henry 'Orator' Hunt, the year he was elected as Preston's Member of Parliament in the sensational election of that year. A part of the building also served as the offices of the Football League for many years at the start of the twentieth century.

The late Preston historian, Marian Roberts, had her home in what had been part of the Castle Hotel, and some of these notes are taken from one of her essays written in 2003, published in the book, *A Preston Mixture*.

CROWN HOTEL, Church Street (1827–1913)

This hotel was one of those that stood where the Miller Arcade now stands, facing south on Church Street. Its late date of 1827 is accounted for by its changing its name from the 'Old Red Lion', following the building of a new Red Lion further along Church Street. When the arcade was erected at the end of the nineteenth century, the Crown Hotel occupied the north-west corner of it, with the tiled entrance doorway still visible next to the magnificent Harris Museum and Art Gallery. Like many of the city centre hotels, this one was also a coaching house, serving all parts of the United Kingdom.

From around 1860 until the early 1870s, the Crown Hotel attempted to compete with others, offering concert hall entertainment, from comedians and ballad singers to the display of human oddities. One such appearance was that of Miss MacDonald, the 'Scottish Giantess', in 1863, the largest woman in the three kingdoms. Precise structural details of Miss MacDonald are not known.

EAGLE AND CHILD, Church Street (eighteenth century–1931)

This Derby family-owned property had its roots in the eighteenth century, and between 1832 and 1840 was known as the 'Church Gates Inn', but the reason for that temporary change isn't known. The eagle and child was the crest of the Derby family, and at one time the inn had a pictorial sign over the doorway showing an eagle's nest with a child inside. Legend has it that the child was the illegitimate son of Sir Thomas Lathom, an ancestor of the house of Stanley and Derby. In fact, this inn was occasionally referred to as 'Lathom House', another Derby connection.

The broad area of Stoneygate next to the Minster is where the Eagle and Child stood, immediately to the east of the Bull and Royal Hotel, another Derby property, and in front of the Old Cock Pit, remembered on an English Heritage Blue Plaque in Stoneygate.

GARTH'S ARMS, Avenham Street (1826–c. 2000)

The Garths were a prominent business family and landowners in the eighteenth and nineteenth centuries, owning many of the Avenham Street properties, certainly on the west side of the street, plus those on Church Street that were ultimately removed to provide access to Avenham Street. Prior to this, access was by way of a narrow passageway in much the same manner as Lancaster Road, Glovers Court and Orchard Street.

Despite the name and ownership of the property, there was never a 'Garth' listed as landlord. However, in 1819, Margaret Garth married Richard Dodgson, and he featured as the landlord in 1831. Whether Margaret was a member of the property-owning family isn't known, but it is likely. Dodgson died in 1833, and in 1834 this house, along with twenty-two other neighbouring lots were auctioned off at the Garth's Arms.

Following the abdication of King Edward VIII in 1936, the Garth's Arms was renamed the Duke of Windsor in his honour. In later years, its name was changed again to 'Gastons' and then 'Noir'.

GEORGE INN and GEORGE INN CONCERT HALL, Friargate (1689–1891)

In 1689, Colonel Bellingham referred to the George Inn in his diary after having partaken in 'stinking oysters' there. Ned Craven was the landlord at the time of the colonel's fishy encounter. The derivation of the inn is something of a mystery, for George I only came to the throne in 1698. I have also seen it referred to on several occasions as the 'George and Dragon', a name that could suggest it is derived from a totally different source. Huge gaps exist in our knowledge, with only two isolated references to it in the 1700s.

While the inn offered residential facilities, particularly useful for those attending markets and agricultural fairs, it wasn't until around 1864 that its use and offerings changed. In that year, the George Inn was taken over by Edward Blackoe, who was intent on building and creating a concert room. This was achieved by using the large facilities to the rear of the inn that had hitherto been used as stabling for horses and storing coaches.

The success of his plans can be seen in the advertisement that he placed in the *Preston Chronicle* in December 1864, when he pointed out that on the opening night 'hundreds of people were refused admission to prevent suffocation'.

At the end of the nineteenth century, and after the erection of the Harris Museum and Art Gallery, it was decided that those properties on east side of Friargate were impeding the view of the new public building and would be demolished. The George Inn was one of them, but a replacement, called the George Hotel, was built on part of old foundations. The new hotel operated for around thirty years, after which the name was adopted by a Church Street public house, the Horse Shoe Inn, and the Friargate–Market Street property became a financial institution.

GREY HORSE, Church Street (1818–present)

This was the early name for a place that became better known as Addison's Wine Bar. At one point it was one of only two thatched inns in Preston, along with the Virgins Inn in Anchor Weind, and in the first quarter of the twentieth century it retained much of its old world interior charm.

Mary Addison was the licencee between 1859 and 1895, having bought the property in 1854, and it is her name that was memorialised in the name of the later wine bar, although, strictly speaking it was a Yates' Wine Lodge. Yates' also had a lodge in the old Sun Inn premises in Main Sprit Weind, so perhaps the name was retained to provide identification. Mary Addison was the sister of Peter and Simon Yates. Today it is again known as Yates' Grey Horse and is a far cry from times past in terms of comfort.

GREY HORSE AND SEVEN STARS, Fishergate (1732–c. 1923)

The popular story about how this public house got its name begins with the knowledge

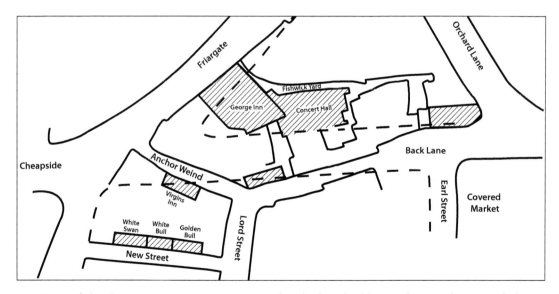

Part of the Corporation regeneration work. The hatched line indicates the amended layout of the area.

The Grey Horse.

that, in the Poor Law Rate Assessment Book of 1732, it was known as the 'White Horse and Seven Stars'. At some point between 1828 and 1832, as a consequence of the effects both of time and the grime-laden atmosphere of industrial Preston, the sign of the White Horse had become grey. Rather than repaint the sign to its original colour, it is said that it was decided to change the name of the pub! True or not, it's a charming story, and in similar fashion to the Borough Tavern, there's a sizeable gap in our knowledge, in this instance from 1732 to the early 1800s. Mrs Beswick, who died in 1810, aged fifty-seven years, is described as the wife of James Beswick, formerly of the 'White Horse', Fishergate.

The house had a good reputation for operating within the law, which helped longstanding landlady Isabella Bibby out in 1876 when she was summoned for serving out of hours when her clock was an hour slow. The case was dismissed because of her unblemished record. Further evidence of this being a valuable and well-run house came the following year, when it was sold for 'something immense', although a precise figure wasn't mentioned.

In the 1891 sale of the business from Dennis Rutter to William McNeil, a detailed inventory of the equipment included in the sale has been found. It included 'four brass spittoons for the front bar parlour'.

In 1923, the Grey Horse was bought by George Toulmin, the owner of the *Preston Guardian*. It was incorporated with the Borough Tavern and became the *Lancashire Evening Post* premises.

KING'S ARMS, Church Street (1732–present)

The King's Arms was one of a number of hotels located on the land now occupied by the Miller Arcade. It was, like some of the others, a coaching house. In 1732, it was noted as the 'King's Arms and Woolpack'. At the comparatively early date of 1827, it was offering entertainment such as the juggling magician, Khia Khan Khruse, from the King's Opera House and Theatre Royal, Drury Lane, London. In an 1871 sale notice, the facilities were

The King's Arms.

described: 'On the ground floor there are excellent ale and spirit vaults with sitting room attached; also a good bar and three parlours attached, with stable and large brewery at the rear of the premises. On the second floor there is a commodious billiard room, a private business room, a sitting room, parlour, ante-room and capital club room. On the third floor there are six good bedrooms. The attics are lofty and so commodious that they may easily be used for bedroom purposes.'

When the property was demolished towards the end of the nineteenth century, a replacement known initially as the 'New King's Arms' was incorporated at the south-east corner of the new Miller Arcade. During the Second World War, it acquired the name 'Long Bar', the derivation of which came from the name of the landlord of the time, Thomas Long. It is now predominantly a young people's bar, featuring heavily in the city's nightlife.

NEW COCK INN, New Cock Yard (1810–1970s)

Until the last few years of the eighteenth century, this inn formed a part of the mansion residence of Thomas Winckley, a member of the gentry who enjoyed nothing more than the high life in London. With the increasing industrialisation of Preston, he decided that it was no longer the place to live, and went to live permanently in the metropolis. The rear portion of his mansion became the New Cock Inn, and its first landlord was William Ascroft, whose son, Robert, went on to become town clerk and formed the company of lawyers R. & W. Ascroft. The first offices for this company were in New Cock Yard, before they moved to Cannon Street and finally Winckley Square.

A cockpit continued to exist in the premises until a fire in 1961 required the removal of the top floor of the property, along with its cock loft and sunken cockpit with handrail partially around the circumference for the convenience of spectators. It was rumoured that cock fights were carried on here long after the sport were officially banned.

OLD COCK INN, Old Cock Yard (1807–c. 1930)
Exactly when the Old Cock Inn originated isn't known, but a recent discovery has revealed that in 1807 it had been called the 'Turf Tavern'. The landlord at the time was Thomas Bradburn, who had been referred to in a Preston race meeting notice as 'Sworn Judge of the Races'. Later, when it was known as the Old Cock Inn, there was a sale of furniture and other household items; these included paintings called *Beeswing*, *Sir Hercules*, *Satirist* and *Coronation*. Enquiries revealed that they were all racehorses. The mare Beeswing was sired by the great Doctor Syntax, seven-times winner of the Preston Gold Cup, whose name also featured in the name of two Preston public houses. Beeswing won an incredible fifty-one races out of the sixty-three events she competed in. Sir Hercules was the offspring of an Epsom Derby winner. Satirist was a racing mare, and Coronation a sire, who by coincidence was a son of Sir Hercules. Coronation had only a few races, including a narrow defeat in the St Leger, and was then retired to stud and exported to Russia.

These details are not conclusive evidence that the Turf Tavern and the Old Cock Inn are synonymous, but there was clearly a keen association with matters of the turf.

OLD LEGS OF MAN, Fishergate (1802–1910)
Standing immediately opposite the site of the old town hall, this Derby family-owned former coaching house probably had its founding in the eighteenth century, although my first record is 1802. The sign in the photograph showed the three legs, which recalled the Derby's connections with the Isle of Man, painted in bright blue with gilded spurs attached to the heels.

Joseph Croft, who was the landlord here in 1821, was one of the pioneers of bath chairs in Preston, a mode of transport that became fashionable with both men and women, and succeeded the elegant sedan chair. Croft had moved to the Red Lion Hotel on Church Street by 1823, where, with greater facilities, he carried on the service.

Between 1841 and 1850, the landlord was William Whittam, who brought with him from the neighbouring Turk's Head public house the brewing skills and facilities he'd used there, supplying not only the needs of his retail customers, but businessmen and families in the wealthier areas of the town, such as Winckley Square. Additional evidence of Joseph Croft taking his bath chair business with him to the Red Lion can be deduced from an advert Whittam placed in the *Preston Chronicle* in September 1844, when he announced that 'he had added to his establishment, Bath Carriages, Gigs, and Saddle Horses'. When Whittam left in 1850, he advertised for sale 'one double and two single bath carriages, one gig, one drag, and four horses'. Later the same year, Whittam opened what was to be known as Glover Street Brewery, the backs of which property were accessible from the long yard next to the entrance to the Old Legs of Man, and which he may have been planning, and perhaps operating, for a period of time.

A sad occurrence took place in 1904 when the landlord, Arthur Aston, attempted to murder his wife by shooting her at the home of a friend of hers. He shot himself dead immediately afterwards. It isn't known if she survived, but the Old Legs was taken over by Arthur's brother, Frederick, who remained until the bank next door acquired the property. At a later date, the property was sold to the family grocers, E. H. Booth, whose shop was next door, and extended to include the acquisition. Eagle-eyed readers will recognise the window to the right of the photograph as being that of Booths, now Waterstone's book retailers.

RED LION HOTEL, Church Street (1809–present)

Although there is doubt as to when this public house first opened, it is thought to have been in 1809. The original Red Lion, on the site of Miller Arcade, remained and was known as the Old Red Lion until 1827, when it was renamed the 'Crown Hotel' and extended into neighbouring property. This one was usually referred to as the 'New' Red Lion and, along with the Old Red Lion, was a coaching house of note. Such is the passage of time that in 1779 the 'Old' Red Lion was itself known as the 'New' Red Lion, there having been a previous 'Red Lyon'.

The name 'Red Lion' has been connected or associated with a neighbouring church in towns up and down the country, and such is the case here, with this one standing directly across from the Minster – the original one was no more than 50 metres closer to the old town hall. However, it is the most popular of all names for public houses, so the possibility of a church and a Red Lion occurring in close proximity is perhaps not unlikely. Its early use is thought to have had a connection with John of Gaunt, the most powerful man in England for much of the fourteenth century.

Following on from the Joseph Croft's bath chair business of the 1820s, the landlord who succeeded him in 1847, Thomas Rainford, was clearly in a business partnership with the undertakers, Brewster and Burrows, and offered the patent 'Shillibeer' mourning coaches, designed to carry the deceased and six passengers. This was in addition to more conventional coaching travel.

As passenger travel developed, the Red Lion became the registered office of the newly created 'Preston Livery and Carriage Company', and they began to offer 'horse-drawn bus travel from the hotel to Fulwood and return'. There were five journeys a day in each direction, 'and arrangements for other routes are being matured'. Unfortunately, the company ran into financial difficulties and didn't survive for long.

The premises of the Red Lion still exist and now operate as a club-type public house, with a younger clientele. The formerly prominent red lion has been painted a pale colour and is far less noticeable.

SHELLEY ARMS HOTEL, Fishergate (1825–c. 1920)

This commercial hotel was demolished in 1920 in order to provide the land for a new Woolworth's store. The entrance, through a curved archway, led into Shelley Arms Yard, and further along the passage was a quantity of stabling for the use of residents

The Old Legs of Man. *Inset:* The small, repainted statue on the front of the Red Lion Hotel.

and visitors. The ground floor was a complicated mix of accommodation, which had been added and amended over the years, emerging further east into Woodcock's Court. There was also further stabling connected to the hotel, accessible from that court.

Around 1830, Lady Francis Shelley, after whom the hotel is said to be named, wrote from her home in Belgravia, London, to organise a celebration for her son's birthday at the hotel. She stated a preference that it should be held on 4 June, for that was her twenty-third wedding anniversary, 'the happiest day of my life'.

Although the earliest date I have for this hotel is 1825, I feel sure it extends further back than that. When it closed down, a commentator in a local paper wrote, 'The end of this ancient hostel, one which, according to ancient custom provided accommodation for man and beast'.

It seems never to have been anything but a well-administered hotel. In the same article to which I referred earlier, it noted that 'the smoke-room of the Shelley's was filled with well-known local gentlemen'.

STANLEY ARMS HOTEL, Lancaster Road (1853–present)

The original Stanley Arms stood on Church Street from, at the latest, 1827 until 1852. At that date it was demolished, along with several other properties, to open up access to Lancaster Road. Hitherto, access had been gained through a narrow passageway. The Earls of Derby, whose family name was Stanley, rebuilt the property on Lancaster Road.

The hotel (*left*) was re-established in one of those built in the 1850s, all of a substantial nature, and many of them remain to this day. The alternative name for this house, which came into being in 1923, was the 'Knowsley Hotel', another reference to the Derby family, Knowsley Hall being the seat of the Stanley family on the outskirts of Merseyside, and now better known as Knowsley Safari Park. It again traded as the Stanley Arms Hotel in 1973. It remains so to this day and still plays a major part in the licensed trade economy.

SUN INN, Main Sprit Weind (1818–present)

Although the earliest date given here is 1818, it is strongly believed that this inn existed in the 1600s. In the southern gable end of the property are the remains of a sun mask, a common addition to houses bearing this name. The rays of the sun have disappeared, however, which is probably evidence that the roof, which was at one time thatched, had more recently been replaced and lowered in height, with the resultant loss of part of the mask.

I have seen Main Sprit Weind variously described as a narrow, dismal, steep and uninviting alleyway, but in times long past it was one of the more desirable places to live, with fashionable houses and coffee gardens. It was, in fact, one of the important routes into the town centre. At its foot was the Syke River, now culverted as far as the River Ribble, and in addition there was also a well at the bottom of the Weind, which served much of the town centre's needs.

A wonderful story was described in a *Preston Chronicle* article of May 1860. The landlord's four-year-old son climbed a ladder leaning against the wall of a

neighbouring property, which was being thatched, and then up another one placed on the roof, eventually reaching the peak of his own roof, where, it was said, he straddled the ridge 'as if riding his cock-horse to Banbury Cross'. His father, Jonathon Westray, managed to reach him and bring him to safety.

During the twentieth century, the Sun Inn (*below left*) operated as a Yates' Wine Bar, and today it continues as the Revolution Bar.

VIRGINS INN, Anchor Weind (1796–1894)

For a period of time, this inn was known as the 'Curriers' Arms'. The likelihood is that it was during the period around 1837 when the landlord was a Mr T. Ascroft, whose principal occupation was as a currier. It is one of the more familiar of the inns and taverns demolished during the late nineteenth century Corporation improvements, thanks to the occasional photograph, but more usually the Edward Beattie paintings. It was thatched to the last, and Beattie's paintings showed the newly built Harris Museum and Art Gallery in the background. This isn't positive proof that both buildings coexisted given a modicum of artistic licence, but it is clear they did. It was one of the last buildings to be demolished during that particular modernisation programme. The Virgins Inn was a firm favourite with ladies visiting the market place due to the hospitality of the final landlady, Jane Lea, who became host along with her husband in 1873, at which point it became known as 'Lea's Virgins' Inn'. Thomas died in 1877, leaving her on her own, and I believe that it sold as many pots of tea as it did beer while the market was in progress.

Despite its apparent small size and quaintness, it is recorded that in 1878, Jane 'entertained to a sumptuous repast the members of the Athenæum Football Club, along with other private friends, to the number of almost sixty'. At the conclusion of the meal, the usual toasts were proposed and responded to, before a band played music and songs were sung until midnight. Perhaps it was bigger than it looked.

WELLINGTON INN, Glovers Court (1839–present)

The Wellington Inn is believed to be the most haunted public house in Preston. Tradesmen working on the premises, who had no prior knowledge of its reputation, have been seen to tremble with fear, blood draining from their faces, at their unexpected experiences. Articles 'flying across the bar' are signs of a disturbance in most public houses, but not at the Wellington. Several occurrences of a varying nature have been witnessed.

The most widely held belief is that the ghost is that of John Alderson, a thirty-year-old workman who was killed here in 1839 during an argument over a debt of one penny. The sad affair left nine children without a father, John having three children and his assailant six. William Bell was 'transported for life' after being convicted of aggravated manslaughter, and told that for some years he would be among the worst classes of those transported.

The Wellington was built expressly as an inn in 1838, and from the start was offering stabling for those attending the market in Preston. At this time there was no vehicular access from Fishergate, merely pedestrian access until some years later, when, like several other streets in the centre of Preston, it was opened up for that purpose. Prior access had been from Avenham Lane alone. Today, the Wellington continues to enjoy a healthy trade. At lunchtimes, the pub is particularly popular with nearby professionals and other office workers taking advantage of the range of simple but highly rated food offerings.

The landlord George Brumley (*left*) with a regular at the Wellington.

Chapter Two

The Outer Circle

In this chapter we are to deal with those hostelries that stood within a circle that has the new Ringway in the north at its outer points. This has been chosen because to the east of its junction with North Road, it follows the old route of Park Road, formerly Scotland Road, while to the west of the North Road junction it follows the old High Street, which was, as is suggested by the name, the highest point in Preston, but also a westward continuation of Park Road.

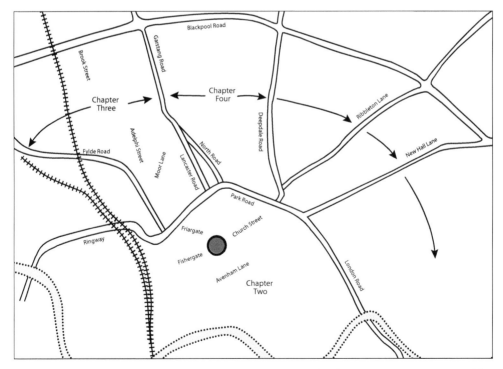

A diagrammatic view of how the chapters are arranged. Chapter one is represented by the red circle, with chapter two all areas south of Ringway and Park Road. Chapters three and four lie west and east of Lancaster Road and Garstang Road.

Ringway continues west to the River Ribble, and so the river, itself the boundary of the city, will form a convenient southern extent of the circle, as far east as London Road. Travelling back towards the city along London Road, everything to the left or west of London Road will be included here, while the eastern side will be included in chapter four.

With a few notable exceptions, the area contained within this circle was the scene of all that happened within the borough in the first thirty years or more of the nineteenth century, with the areas outside of the circle being developed in the years beyond.

Finally, and having regard to those readers who are not so conversant with the layout of Preston in times past, the Ringway and its extension to the east should make it simpler to envisage. I hope it does!

ALBION HOTEL, Church Street (1832–1915)

The Albion Hotel was the original name of the premises that later became known as the Imperial Hotel, and then the Royal Hotel. In 1881, during a court case, it was referred to in the local press as the 'Glass Barrel Hotel'. While just a single pane of glass had been broken, resulting in the court hearing, criminal damage on a large scale was not an uncommon occurrence here, particularly when conducted as part of 'electioneering sports'. It is ironic that a place that changed its name so often, probably to avoid bad publicity, had been the residence prior to 1832 of one of the Grimshaw family, as well as Thomas Batty Addison – the former local politicians of note, the latter a local lawyer and recorder.

The entrance at the eastern side of the hotel led to a large courtyard, at the far end of which were the stables, while off to the left of the stables was a smithy, whose services were used by many tradesmen in the town. On the right-hand side of the courtyard was a huge building that had been used from time to time by groups such as the Spinners' Institute and a militia group as a storeroom. In the 1840s and 1850s, it was used by the hotel as a low-class concert hall and singing room. At a time when there were grave concerns about the harm these places were causing young people, many of them little more than fourteen or fifteen years of age, this concert hall featured in a report prepared by those attempting to have such places controlled, or preferably closed down.

It is interesting to note that, in the report, the room was described as 30 yards by 10 yards, and capable of holding between 800 and 1,000 persons.

ANGEL INN, Lune Street (1838–present)

There have been two Angel Inns in Preston, one a short-lived establishment in Angel Court in the Back Lane area, and this one (*opposite above*).

This Angel Inn had a rather shaky start when the first landlord, John Stock, a corn merchant, went bankrupt. But following this, the inn experienced a long settled period under the Nightingale family, enjoying trade from those attending the markets at the Corn Exchange. In the late nineteenth and twentieth centuries, it took similar advantage of those attending the huge range of attractions, from Victorian exhibitions and concerts to the performances of Paul Robeson, Bing Crosby, the jazz bands of Aker Bilk and Chris Barber, and many others, as well as orchestral concerts.

During the nineteenth century, and possibly later, the landlords of the Angel would tender for, and often win, the supply of catering facilities at suitable events in the Exchange. In one such instance in 1878, the newspaper report following the event said, 'Mr. W. T. Bilsborough of the Angel Inn, Lune Street, had charge of the more exhilarating refreshments.'

Saturday night dances at the Corn Exchange, more familiarly known as the Public Hall, were often preceded by a visit to this inn, but gone are the things that drew the population to its doors, and a portion of the Corn Exchange has been converted into a public house, becoming competition for the Angel Inn. The Angel, however, continues as an important part of the city nightlife.

ANGLERS' INN, Pole Street (1839–1960s)

The Anglers' (*below right*) was the first public house that Matthew Brown owned; the man who went on to own and supply a huge estate of houses, mainly in the Lancashire area, from his Preston, and later Blackburn-based, breweries.

This house was particularly remembered for its unique stone statue of an angler above the Pole Street entrance. It was said to be a likeness of his friend, Tom Banks, with whom he shared a passion for fishing. For well over 100 years, his brewery produced a strong winter brew called 'Old Tom', and a correspondent recently told me that that also was a reference to her ancestor, the same Tom Banks. For years the brew was advertised using the face of a cat, with an invitation to 'Try our Old Tom'!

The entrance to the Anglers' Inn from Pole Street also had a large metal

lampshade over the door. It was said that the lampshade had been made on the back of a lorry during the Preston Guild Festivities Trades Procession in 1862, by a small team of metalworkers, headed by a man in armour on horseback, representing Vulcan. During the same year, there was a huge archway constructed outside the premises in Pole Street, extending to the building line on the opposite side of the street. By this time, Matthew Brown had built his brewery on the corner diagonally opposite the Anglers', and I suspect that he had been instrumental in either its construction, sponsorship, or both. All other similar archways were positioned at significant points in the town, usually at points connected with the processions. Certainly in those days, Preston Guilds, which have occurred every twenty years since 1328, were occasions when businessmen could make a statement, and tradesmen could display and celebrate their trades and skills.

It is understood that at the end of its life in the late 1960s, the Anglers' Inn, having resisted the urge to modernise, was virtually unchanged in terms of decor and layout from its early Victorian days.

ARKWRIGHT ARMS, Stoneygate (1851–1892)

In the year 1768, Richard Arkwright was a lodger here with the headmaster of the grammar school. It was here that he perfected his invention and ran the first feasible spinning machine. The rest, as they say, is cotton history. The building had from 1728 been the property of the Corporation, and the residence of the headmaster of the neighbouring Preston Grammar School. It later became a public house, before finding use as a men's hostel in the 1890s. At one point, the building on the right of Arkwright House was used as the tavern, but the reason for that isn't clear. This would also answer why the address was at one time given as No. 12 Stoneygate, and at others as Nos 1, 2 and 3 Shepherd Street.

Sixty years after the creation of the Temperance Society, and after the death of Joseph Livesey, drinking and drunkenness began to soar again. In the early 1890s, a Vigilante Committee was formed to oppose the granting of licences to those places that had earned a reputation for unruliness, or allowing the wrong type of person to frequent them, such as thieves or prostitutes. The Arkwright Arms was one of them. In 1892, the licence was acquired by Arthur Margerison, who was a soap manufacturer in Preston. In some accounts he went by the name Caleb Margerison, but whether he was one in the same man, or a relative from the family firm isn't known. After he had remodelled the inn into a model lodging house, he moved to the Isle of Man, taking much of the fine old wooden panelling from the premises with him. He was not one of the vigilantes, but someone who was wealthy enough to take the place over with the sole intent of closing it down.

In the 1970s, the property almost became the subject of a demolition order, but a group calling itself the Friends of Arkwright House appealed for funds and saved it. It went on to be used by, among others, Age Concern.

BEAR'S PAW, Church Street (1760–present)

These premises were originally known by this name, although for large periods they have been known as the 'Grapes Hotel'. In the early 1800s, there was another 'Grapes'

The Bear's Paw.

or 'Grapes and Punchbowl' in what is now Tithebarn Street, and the Bear's Paw acquired that name some years after the original one was demolished and replaced by the Imperial Hotel at the corner of Lord Street, opposite the Waggon and Horses.

The Bear's Paw is said to have been the first place that Matthew Brown brewed beer in the 1830s, in a building at the rear of the public house. It was likely to have been for only a short period, for he continued to do so at the Anglers' Inn before building his brewery close by.

During the last major refurbishment here around the year 1987, builders reported that there was evidence that there had been a building here for a lot longer than my first record of a landlord in 1818. Wooden beams dating back to 1707 were found, but they concluded that it was older than that. Handmade bricks of the type made in the Tudor period were used in the construction of it, which could date it back to around 1600.

How long it had been a tavern prior to 1818 isn't known, but it is recorded that in 1760 this was the home of the Preston Landed Interest Club, which met every Saturday afternoon. It was reported that 'in those days the Bear's Paw was a quiet and orthodox house – a calm, serene place, resorted to by quiet men fond of gin and water, and long, church-warden pipes'. They would discuss the quality and the quantity of their property, the cash they were worth, and other matters, but all directly related to money.

As early as 1875, there were newspaper reports of this house being 'a den of thieves', and little was to change for 100 years or more, with periods when it was a particularly

Black-a-Moor Head Hotel.

troubled licensed property. However, today it is operated by a small operator, whose approach is quite different to that of its larger competitors, and it thrives in an orderly manner mainly as a purveyor of beer.

BLACK-A-MOOR HEAD HOTEL, Lancaster Road (1831–present)

This represents one of those public houses that have retained the same name throughout their existence, and yet their address has changed over the years from Chadwick's Orchard, to Lancaster Street, to Lancaster Road South, and finally Lancaster Road. It was recorded in one instance as being in Ormskirk Road but, despite the possibility, it's probably erroneous.

This house, standing at the corner of Old Vicarage, opposite the Covered Market, was built for purpose around 1830. On 1 January 1831, it was advertised for let for a term of years, together with its stables, cattle pens and brewhouse. The house itself is a substantial building that originally had a dining room on the first floor measuring 44 feet in length, running at right angles to Lancaster Road. It can be deduced from this snippet of information that the proposed use of the hotel was to be for the service of visiting farmers to what was then Chadwick's Orchard, a huge plot of land that it faced on the other side of Lancaster Road. On the second floor, the advertisement described seven bedrooms and a barracks room, a reminder of the time when public houses were obliged to house members of the militia. In a further advertisement in

August 1831, there was a boast that 'a considerable Fat Cattle Market, on Thursday, is already established, and which is still increasing'.

The prime interest of its first landlord, Mr Pemberton, isn't known, but from 1838, and for much of the next sixty years, it was overseen by the Ashcroft family, who were also farmers. The first one was Thomas Ashcroft, but thereafter it seems that successors to the role of landlord here was reserved for the next in line named Daniel, whether he was the eldest son or not. Perhaps it was coincidence?

Sales in the yard of these premises ranged from the sale in 1877 of 'sixty Mountain Ponies, direct from Iceland', together with 'a lot of fat Iceland Sheep', to 'fifty tons of good Horse Manure'.

A notable exception to the Black-a-Moor's Head's farming connection occurred in 1890, when James Trainer, the 'Prince of Goalkeepers' and member of the renowned 'Old Invincibles' Preston North End football team, became the landlord. In 1888/89, the Preston team had won the inaugural Football League competition without losing a game, and the FA Cup without conceding a goal, a feat never equalled. He was only here for a couple of years, but went on to run other public houses in the town. Several of his football colleagues did the same, presumably making the most of their notoriety.

Its situation in a busy part of the city, and close to the Covered Market, ensures the continuance of a good trade for this well-known house.

BLACK HORSE HOTEL, Friargate (1796–present)

The Black Horse Hotel (*overleaf*) is arguably the most popular public house in Preston, if for no other reason than its Grade II listed interior; a status awarded mainly on account of its wonderful, semi-circular ceramic vault bar. People with only a mild interest in local history travel long distances to be able to say that they've seen it. The small, original rooms are also preserved, as is the old leaded-light interior glasswork panelling.

Not many people realise that the building we see today is relatively young, having replaced an older building in the 1890s. The older building changed hands in 1797, and so will precede that date. It also enjoyed, for a time in the 1800s, the more exotic name of 'Black Horse and Rainbow Hotel'. In the early 1800s, a narrow alleyway known as Plant's Court, or Rowland Plant's Court, provided access to Starch House Square and Chadwick's Orchard, until adjacent properties were demolished to construct Orchard Street, leaving the old alleyway, better known these days as Lowthian Street or Black Horse Yard.

The 1890s building was constructed as a small hotel to designs by local architect J. A. Seward. Throughout the twentieth century it enjoyed notoriety as the only public house in Preston to have three postal addresses; the most traditional one was Friargate, but it also had No. 1 Orchard Street, and No. 1 Lowthian Street, as a back up.

The fact that it was built as a small hotel probably accounts for the interior furnishings, which are far superior to those likely to be encountered in street corner taverns of similar vintage. Situated adjacent to the marvellous Hippodrome, it perhaps sought to offer accommodation to the thespians. The Star and Garter on Brook Street also had entrances from Byrom Street and Brougham Street as well as Brook Street, but they possibly weren't postal addresses.

The first-floor bar overlooks both Friargate and Orchard Street and was known as 'Peter's Bar' throughout the twentieth century, after the 1904 landlord, John S. Peters. It has been totally revamped, and is now an eatery called 'Graze 'n' Grog'. Huge amounts of money have been expended on the modernisation of the cellars, and so proud are they that inspections are invited from the public, by appointment or when time permits. Similarly, visitors are invited to do a bit of 'tapping and venting' when it's practicable. This could give this hotel a further uniqueness.

(YE OLDE) BLUE BELL HOTEL, Church Street (1716–present)

A sale by auction notice in the *Preston Chronicle* in April 1840 described the house as having 'extensive stables, out-buildings and yard'. The fourteen cottage properties in Blue Bell Yard, at the side of the tavern, were for sale as part of the package, and the land and gardens associated with the public house ran back as far as Queen Street. The property was owned at this time by the Trustees of Hutton School, and was the subject of a lease of forty-one years from May 1812.

When you learn of the extent of the land connected with this property, it becomes less surprising to imagine that wrestling matches involving up to forty contestants a day took place here, with prizes in 1841 ranging from 2s 6d (12.5p) to £4 for heavyweights, and 2s 6d to £2 10s (£2.50) for lightweights. Contestants would come to Preston from Kendal, Cockermouth, Millom, and elsewhere. In fact, in the tournament in June 1841, thirteen of the twenty heavyweights were from outside the Preston area.

In August 1881, Annie, the sixteen-year-old daughter of landlord Alfred Ratcliffe, was violently murdered in the best parlour of the nearby Sir Walter Scott Inn, located on North Road at its junction with Lord's Walk.

Having served Annie and her fiancé with bottles of lemonade, the landlady's attention was almost immediately attracted by the sound of breaking glass. She rushed into the parlour to find blood everywhere, Annie's throat cut, and her attacker sitting 'sullen, but unexcited' in a corner of the room. A caesarean was performed on the pregnant Annie, but despite the child being born alive, it died within five minutes. She was killed by John Aspinall Simpson, the father of her child. They were due to be married later the same day. The case, needless to say, provoked great excitement in the borough, but Aspinall pleaded guilty and was later hanged.

While the Blue Bell still exists, it has found itself a little isolated in a part of Preston that was due to undergo massive alterations and development, before an eleventh-hour cancellation of the project. Perhaps future development will breathe new life into this charming old tavern.

(THE) CONTINENTAL HOTEL, South Meadow Lane (1911–present)

Strictly speaking, this currently vibrant hotel was outside the remit of my original research, having only been built in 1911. However, it was a replacement for the Bowling Green Inn, on whose land it was built, although not on the same footprint.

The land that comprised the Pleasure Boat Inn and the Bowling Green Inn had been purchased by Thomas Croft, the builder. Thomas Croft was the father-in-law of Sam Thomson, a member of Preston North End's Old Invincible team of 1888/89 (*see the Black-a-Moor Head Hotel, page 32*). Initially, Sam Thomson went to the Bowling Green Inn, but it would appear to have been a deliberately temporary arrangement, for while he was there, Croft & Company were building the Continental Hotel.

It is of interest to note that the neighbouring Pleasure Boat Inn and Bowling Green Inn had been rivals in the apparently lucrative but seasonal boat hire business, and the boathouse connected with the Bowling Green Inn was preserved on the westerly side of the new building. Croft also built half a dozen houses on South Meadow Lane, adjacent to the hotel, and these surprisingly flat-roofed properties are still there.

The Pleasure Boat Inn and the Bowling Green Inn were both closed down by Croft when the Continental opened, and the former has enjoyed an afterlife as a pair of bay-fronted cottages, together with the adjacent Mini Centre, opened around 1970 to offer services to owners of the iconic Minis of that era.

For many years, there was a separate café business associated with the Continental, operated by a family called Worden. It was always referred to as the 'Café Continental', and many will remember the ice cream stall that stood close to the entrance during suitable weather. Today, the Continental is one of the more successful out of city centre venues, offering live music and an eclectic mixture of similar live art entertainment. It runs extremely ambitious and regular beer festivals, with over 100 ales, lagers and ciders featured. The festivals are often held in May, and if the weather obliges the ambience and views along the River Ribble are difficult to beat. It has also earned an enviable reputation for its extensive and imaginative food offerings.

CORPORATION ARMS, Lune Street/Wharfe Street (1824–c. 1967)

Although there have been many public houses erected by the Corporation of Preston,

Above: The Continental Hotel. *Below:* The Corporation Arms.

this was the only one to bear the Corporation's name. It endured a sad and serious history; perhaps the best-known example was during the period of the Chartist Riots of 1842, when the Riot Act was read before five male millworkers were shot dead. A sixth man died later of his wounds. The front face of the Corporation Arms was in the line of the militia's aim, and marks were made by the balls fired from muskets that were visible until the inn was demolished around 1967 to make way for the Ring Road. A memorial depicting the incident has been erected on Lune Street, but unfortunately the protagonists are facing in totally the wrong direction.

An 1833 advertisement claimed that the inn had stabling for forty horses, so there was plenty of opportunity to benefit from the trade presented by its presence across the street from the Corn Exchange and its attendant markets.

A serious accident befell the Corporation Arms in 1853, during the time of the mill closures, with many people out of work and destitute. There was a weekly meeting here when workers who found themselves in such circumstances would be paid a stipend by their union. On the day of the accident, there were up to 300 people in the first floor room when the flooring, without the slightest warning, gave way under the weight. The room was above the coach house, close to the stable yard, and those in the room were plunged into it. Although there were many broken bones and crush injuries, as well as less serious injuries, there was only one fatality.

CRAVEN HEIFER, North Road (1825–1967)

The Craven Heifer must have been built adjacent to a spring, for in its early days there was a pump in the yard of the inn by which water was raised to sell to the neighbourhood. There was a similar one, known as the 'Park Pump' in nearby Pump Street; a well was placed over this in 1827. Presumably, this gave a distinct advantage to the inn, and a unique character to the ale brewed there.

The Craven Heifer stood at the junction of a number of roads, namely Park Road, North Road, Walker Street and Meadow Street, and stood facing north along the road of that name. It was a noticeable if unremarkable building that stood in the centre of a large circle of competitors in all the roads mentioned above, and the side streets off them. None were closer than the Apollo Inn at the corner of Walker Street and North Road.

The final landlord at the Craven Heifer was Tom Roberts, a former Preston North End footballer, who was a high-scoring favourite with the fans of the club. A poster on the front of the building indicated that he was trading in his name. The inn closed shortly before the Second World War, with Roberts moving to the Stephenson's Arms in East Street.

EXCHANGE HOTEL, Fox Street (1867–present)
FOX AND GRAPES HOTEL, Fox Street (1841–present)

Despite their presence together as neighbours for a considerable period of time, these two taverns have a surprisingly under-recorded past. While the Fox and Grapes Hotel has retained its name for most of its long life, the Exchange Hotel began its days as the Oddfellows Arms in 1851. In 1861, when the landlord from the Fox and Goose in

Bolton Street West took over here, he seems to have brought Reynard's name with him, renaming the place the Fox Street Tavern.

Both of these establishments drew trade from the Corn Exchange at the foot of Fox Street, and the second change of name in 1867 would seem to recognise that most of the deals done at the markets in the Corn Exchange were finalised in the Exchange Hotel.

Both properties exist to this day, but their character has changed dramatically. Firstly, the Exchange became a younger person's cocktail bar, and then the owners of the Exchange took control of the Fox and Grapes in 2013. They converted it into a similar venue and now operate them in competition with one another.

FARMERS' ARMS, Back Lane (Market Street) (1846–1980s)

It's a surprise that the earliest date is as late as it is. I have a record of another beerhouse in Back Lane in 1851 called the 'Farmers' Home' with a different landlord to the Farmers' Arms, so maybe the history of one of them extended further back. For a historic market town to have no Farmers' Arms before 1846 would seem a strange omission.

Be that as it may, the most recent Farmers' Arms, latterly known as the Jolly Farmer, was an impressive building at the junction of Market Street and Orchard Street. Its predecessor stood in a similar position, but a couple of properties away from the junction. When the hotel was residential, it had a large number of letting rooms, but the most unusual feature at the Farmers' Arms was that the stables were situated several floors above ground level, having a series of ramps from one floor to another to allow the horses to gain access.

GEORGE HOTEL (former HORSE SHOE HOTEL), Church Street (1818–1990s)

These premises were in existence in 1818 at the latest and were known as the Horse Shoe Hotel. In its early days, the hotel included the entrance gate that can just be seen on the right of the photograph (*above right*), and the floors above that entrance would suggest that the hotel offered accommodation for travellers and stabling for six horses. In a sale notice of February 1883, there was mention of a 'brewery and other building having been recently built on land there', although there is no doubt they had been brewing their own ale for years before that date. From 1883, when Squire Robert Gray and his wife Elizabeth Mary were running the hotel, it would appear they were brewing for wholesaling to other outlets. It was known as Church Street Brewery, and attempts were made to sell off the brewing concern as a separate entity later that same year. Whether they were successful isn't known.

Like several other leading hotels and taverns in Preston in the 1890s, this one was operated by former members of the Preston North End Old Invincibles team of 1888/89. This one featured in the lives of two members of that team, and another player who only played after that memorable season.

In 1894, James Trainer, formerly of the Black-a-Moor Head on Lancaster Road and the Lamb Hotel, Church Street, moved to this hotel for a period of three years. He was followed by William Greer, the odd one out of the three men, but he only stayed a few months and was succeeded by George 'Geordie' Drummond, who, despite his nickname, was a Scot from Leith, Edinburgh. Another Scot to run this hotel was Belle Webster, the long-standing licencee from 1967 to 1991. 'Firm but fair' was her motto, which one would hope was the motto of many of her long-standing customers – prison staff from their close neighbours, Preston Prison.

The Horse Shoe adopted the name George Hotel in 1926 when the George Hotel at the junction of Friargate and Market Street, close to the market place, ceased to trade. Although no longer trading, the George Hotel building still features in the Church Street landscape as an extension to the successful Ted Carter fishing tackle empire.

GOLDEN CROSS HOTEL,
Lancaster Road (1807–present)

The Golden Cross (*below right*) continues to trade from its position opposite the City Hall and Covered Market, but it hasn't always been there. Its original address was in the Shambles, which was separated from Lancaster Road by Molyneux Square. I have a record of a sale of Whitechapels, gigs, phaetons, and other carriages, plus fifty horses, 'in a spacious yard behind Mr Rainford's Golden Cross, Shambles', and I have reached the conclusion that it was close to where the Stanley Arms Hotel stands now, for at the time there was no other open space behind the properties that would fit the description.

In the mid-1850s, the Derby family built many substantial properties on the east side of Lancaster Road, and Molyneux Square and the Shambles were incorporated into it. The replacement Golden Cross Hotel enjoyed some continuity by William Hesmondhalgh, the landlord, moving from one to the other.

The Kendal Castle.

The new building was certainly equipped to deal with the farming fraternity, for off the yard at the back of the premises, and extending beyond several of its neighbouring properties, were two large loose boxes, a two-storey coach house and stabling for at least a dozen horses, with a substantial hay loft above them. Also off the yard was a two-storey brewhouse.

The bulk of the upper floors have not been fully utilised for some time, but planning permission has just been granted to convert it into residential flats, with the licensed portion continuing to trade.

KENDAL CASTLE, Ladyman Street (1856–c. 2005)

There were originally two public houses at or close to the junction of Good Street and Ladyman Street. The one on the corner was originally the Oddfellows Arms, and adjoining it in Ladyman Street was the Kendal Castle; both were simple beerhouses. There were tensions between succeeding landlords as they strove to obtain a full licence to serve spirits. But the magistrates were reluctant to issue one to both houses, and took the easy way out by denying both the privilege. On one notable occasion, just before the 1864 Brewster Sessions, the landlord of the Oddfellows went to his neighbour and sought his agreement that if he did not apply for a spirit licence, then neither would he, thereby saving them both some money. He got that agreement, but ignored it, applied himself and succeeded. This despite being a considerably smaller house, a fact that was pointed out by the landlady of the Kendal Castle at the following year's sessions when she said, 'You could have got their pub inside mine, plus we've got a Clubroom.' She failed to impress the magistrates sufficiently.

The Lamb Hotel.

Both houses brewed their own ale, and competition was fierce between them on that account as well, with the brewer at the Oddfellows, who was the brother-in-law of the landlord, embarking on a marketing project rarely seen in Preston at the time. Such was his intent to impress on the public that 'it was an Important Fact that his beer was unrivalled in the town' that in the census of 1871, the public house was noted as being called 'The Important Fact'. The name of the brewer was William Braithwaite. He set up a brewery close by called Euston Street Brewery and supplied several nearby inns and taverns, but not the Kendal Castle. He also advertised in the local press that 'it was an Important Fact that he could supply Private Families with small casks, containing from three to nine gallons each'.

The last record for the Oddfellows was in 1910, when the Kendal Castle extended into the property of its erstwhile adversary. It remained in solitude for the better part of the next 100 years, eventually closing its doors around 2005. A tragic event occurred in 1962 with the murder of the landlady, Elsie Salter. On a Saturday in May of that year, a party of racegoers set out for Thirsk races in Yorkshire from the Kendal Castle. As the coach entered Thirsk, it was stopped by the police and Elsie's husband, William, was taken by them back to Preston. It was found that after closing the pub after the lunchtime session, a man called Bernard McCrory had secreted himself in the gent's toilets, later emerging to attack and kill Mrs Salter. He suffered from a mental illness, and was angry that Mrs Salter had denied him a loan of £5. This, sadly, was his revenge.

LAMB HOTEL, Church Street (pre-1818–c. 2000)
Prior to the Brewster Sessions of 1874, this house had traded under the name 'Holy

Lamb Hotel'. At these sessions the word 'Holy' was dropped and the new name adopted. There were individuals in the town that thought the word 'holy' was inappropriate when used in such a way, and it would appear they got their way. It wasn't the first 'Holy Lamb' in Preston, the Borough Tavern on Fishergate having been known by that name in earlier years.

Quite how far back the history of this inn extends isn't clear, but there is little doubt that it does precede 1818. In 1832, after a period of seven years when the landlord had been the impressively named Launcelot Lawrenson, an advertisement appeared in a January edition of the *Preston Chronicle* announcing a sale at the livery stables, which were contiguous to the hotel, of his valuable stud of at least four horses, plus gigs, harnesses, saddles, bridles and other articles. Presumably, the livery stables were the ones on the south side of Church Street, close to the Blue Bell Inn, which were opposite the long gone Patten House, home of the Derby family when they resided in Preston.

Shortly after the departure of Mr Lawrenson, a surgeon from Whitworth, W. T. Hartley, 'set up shop' at the Holy Lamb. An announcement declared that he practised all the various branches of surgery, and that he is 'the oldest practitioner in bone setting of the Whitworth Branch. N.B. Ulcers, Cancers, Fistulas, green and old wounds, perfectly cured. All sorts of Whitworth Rubbing Bottles, Salves, on sale.'

In 1893, this became another public house to be tenanted by Preston North End goalkeeper James Trainer. He'd arrived from the Black-a-Moor Head, and was to move on to the neighbouring George Hotel the following year.

In the last quarter of the twentieth century, the Lamb Hotel became the home of folk, blues, jazz and other genres of music, and the ground-floor windows could often be seen to be reverberating to the sound from within. In that respect, Preston lost an important cultural venue.

MARKET INN, Back Lane (Market Street) (1869–present)

Between the years 1861 and 1866, and possibly extended at both of those extremities, there was a Market Inn in Orchard Street. Very few people know of its former existence, immediately to the rear of the Black Horse Hotel, and on the other corner of Lowthian Street (Black Horse Yard). It occupied the premises that come to a narrow point, and is currently used as a health food shop.

Its replacement, around 1869, was opened as a beerhouse. At the 1874 Brewster Sessions, a licence to sell excisable liquors was applied for. This, along with several adjacent properties in both Back Lane and Orchard Street, owned by Windermere-based Martin Bailey. Landlady Mrs Jane Towers rented the inn in addition to three adjoining cottages in Black Horse Yard, as well as a building set up as a brewhouse and storeroom. She also rented a further storeroom as a stable for five horses and equine equipment. Mrs Towers lived in one of the cottages, leaving the four bedrooms in the inn to be let to a maximum of eleven visiting farmers.

The inn was situated a mere 20 metres from the New Covered Market, and in a later attempt to gain a spirits licence, it was argued that if there was a call for two licensed houses, namely the Farmers' Arms and the Black-a-Moor Head Hotel 'when

Inside the Market Inn. *Inset:* The Market Inn's fireplace.

it was merely a lad's playground', then there must be a case for a third one after the construction of the new market area. This was a reference to when this area was called Chadwick's Orchard, a huge area that had formerly been used intermittently for visiting fairs and circuses. By 1883, a spirit licence had still not been granted, and the new tenant, Edmund Gee, tried once more with the same application. By this time, he was boasting that the inn has eleven bedrooms, rather than room for eleven lodgers; whether it was an error in reporting or new accommodation was provided isn't known. He was again unsuccessful.

Today, the Market Inn provides a service not only for the market, its traders and its visitors, but to those who want to enjoy a compact, comfortable, well-maintained inside area in which to relax, but also, when the weather allows, the ability to choose to sit outdoors in a very French café-style manner.

OLD DOG INN, Church Street (1715–present)

It is believed that this old coaching house has been on its current site since around 1732, and possibly as early as 1715. It is maintained that a former Old Dog, lower down Church Street to the east, had a history extending back into the seventeenth century. In 1690, for instance, Colonel Bellingham referred in his diaries to spending time 'at ye Dogg'. There are records of the post-1715 inn having stables with a capacity to hold sixty horses, so in the days when land travel was exclusively by road, the animated scenes in the vicinity of inns of this nature must have been spectacular.

The Old Dog Inn.

The Pleasure Boat Inn has since been converted into two cottages.

It has to be remembered that before 1800, the only entrance to Preston from the south was into Church Street, close to the prison. As a consequence of its proximity to the Preston residence of the Derby family at Patten House, the Old Dog was the most patronised inn after the Bull and Royal Hotel by the acquaintances and visiting guests of the Derby family, especially when the Preston Races were on.

It is interesting to note that the Old Dog Inn has a connection with early Wesleyan Methodism. Mrs Walmsley, who was the landlady from 1745 until 1776, formed a friendship with Martha Thompson, who is claimed to be the first of the earliest Methodists in Preston. They attended sermons together in places as far away as East Lancashire, and their passion inspired William, the son of Widow Walmsley, to be ordained into the church. They regularly held meetings and services on the first floor of the inn, and an English Heritage Blue Plaque outside the Old Dog Inn commemorates these facts today. It is believed that John Wesley kept his horse in the stables here when he visited Preston.

PLEASURE BOAT INN, Ribbleside (1859–1910)

This inn enjoyed not a long life, but an interesting one. Like its close neighbour, the Bowling Green Inn, it stood close to the north bank of the River Ribble, and they both added the hiring of pleasure boats to the usual purpose of an inn. Extensive landing stages existed in a fashion that found them meeting one another on the riverbank, and competition was fierce between the two of them.

At the Pleasure Boat Inn, for two-thirds of its fifty-one-year known existence, the landlord was John Crook. Both he and his son, also John, were boatbuilders on the premises adjacent to the inn, from which they supplied both themselves and the public with boats of various types. John Crook senior was also well known for his many exploits in saving people who were in danger of drowning. Boats could be hired by anybody with the money, but the nature of this tidal river presented serious dangers to people with little or no knowledge of such hazards. In all, he was credited with saving the lives of no less than thirty-two people. For saving the lives of three Blackburn residents, he was presented with a memento of the occasion by the residents of that town, much to the chagrin of the Corporation in his home town. They had been too slow to respond to his outstanding bravery, but then tried to arrange for the presentation to be made in Preston. Blackburn would have none of it. They presented him with a medal on behalf of the Humane Society, suitably inscribed, together with a testimonial that was described as being 'of exquisite penmanship, illuminated, and handsomely framed'. His wife was presented with a china tea service. At this point, he had saved twenty-three people, and went on to add nine more to the total.

Flooding was a constant threat after severe storms, and during one of the worst of these in 1866, there were reports of barrels of beer, wine and sherry being washed out of the flooded cellars, and carried far downstream. By the year 1911, the inn was in the ownership of local builder Thomas Croft, as was the neighbouring Bowling Green Inn. The latter was demolished and the new Continental Hotel was built on adjacent land. The licence for the former was not renewed. The public house has since been converted into two cottages, and the boathouse is now a car servicing facility.

The bright and airy restaurant and bar inside the Railway Hotel (recently renamed Station Inn).

RAILWAY HOTEL, Butler Street (1861–present)

Although it now trades as the Station Inn, the inn or tavern in Butler Street, is just one of several that once packed the street margins. Five inns or beerhouses on the west side of the street were demolished in the 1870s to facilitate the widening of the rail lines as the railway advanced and trade brought by it increased. In addition to these five was the Railway Hotel on the eastern side. The Queen's Hotel and the North Union Railway Hotel were on opposite sides of Butler Street at its entrance from Fishergate, with the latter of those two being demolished at around the same time as the five in the street itself.

In 1878, probably as a consequence of its competitors having been demolished, the Railway Hotel, which had previously been just a beerhouse, was completely rebuilt on the same footprint and considerably enlarged. It was also granted a full licence to sell spirits. In 1883, the hotel was advertised to let, with the facilities being described as 'having fifteen bedrooms, superior household accommodation, a large Club Room and Sitting Room, and three bar parlours'. Applications were to be made to the Matthew Brown Brewery in Pole Street, evidently the owners.

Throughout the twentieth century and into the twenty-first, it has continued to offer residential accommodation, but on a more modest basis. An advertisement in the 1960s announced a 'New Buffet Bar' and a charmingly decorated and refurnished Cocktail Lounge. A more recent refurbishment has created a public house with two personas; the front lounge and dining area being open and brightly lit through large windows, with a traditional bar and games room to the rear.

REGATTA INN, Fishergate Hill (1837–1914)

The Regatta Inn is likely to have gained its name following the inaugural Preston Regatta that took place on its doorstep in 1833. It had previously been called the Little Bridge Inn after an adjacent bridge over the River Syke, a tributary of the River Ribble that is now totally culverted. It is further thought that prior to the Little Bridge Inn, this pub, or another property on the same ground, was the White Horse referred to in the court leet records of 1686, when landlord William Wearden was required to 'Scour the ditch belonging to the White Horse near to the Water Side'. The Regatta Inn was Corporation-owned, and towards the end of the 1830s, Matthew Brown, local wholesale brewer of note, got involved with the management of the place, despite having just constructed the Anglers' Arms in Pole Street, where he was the landlord for many years. In 1837, the riverside property had been advertised to let, by ticket, on the condition that the landlord would alter and enlarge the premises, at his own expense. Matthew Brown was probably brought in to provide the expertise, possibly the finance and ultimately the beer, although in the early days it was brewed on the premises here as well.

Standing as it did by the side of a tidal river, it was often subject to flooding, although reports of damage suffered were nothing like as frequent, or as serious as that suffered by other public houses further upstream. The Regatta Inn became a victim of road widening in 1914, when the new bridge over the Ribble to Penwortham was constructed.

SPREAD EAGLE HOTEL, Lune Street (1807–1960s)

It is believed that there was another Spread Eagle in nearby Chapel Walks in the eighteenth century. Furthermore, that tavern is believed to have been known as the 'Duke of Cumberland' and 'Mattie's Whim'. The Duke of Cumberland was an anti-Catholic victor of the 1745 uprising, and Mattie Whiteside, a Catholic supporter and the landlord's wife at the time, removed the name from the side of the building. The landlord explained that it was 'Mattie's Whim', and the name apparently stuck.

When one Spread Eagle ceased to trade and the other commenced isn't known, but I'm persuaded to think it was around 1807 at the latest. Several interesting characters ran the Spread Eagle in the 1800s, but none more so than John Dellabella, the son of an Italian immigrant. They were, like one or two other immigrants from Italy, tradesmen in the art of picture framing and gilding, and Dellabella senior practised his profession in Lune Street also.

Between 1851 and 1862, I encountered a number of references to a 'Market Tavern' in Lune Street, but was unable to locate it. Then I chanced upon an auction poster dated 1877, in which it advertised for sale 'a Public House and Market Tavern', the Spread Eagle Hotel. The answer lies in the fact that directly across the street from the hotel was the Corn Exchange, at which were held several markets. Beerhouses would open at five o'clock in the morning for the benefit of traders and others in those circumstances, and it would seem that a part of the Spread Eagle Hotel, or perhaps a separate building adjacent to it, and known as the 'Market Tavern' was operating as such. Further evidence was taken from the *Preston Chronicle* advertisement in April 1877, when it referred in the sale notice that described the sale of 'the Fully-licensed

St John's Brigade outside the Spread Eagle Hotel.

A drawing of the Theatre Tavern from the 1800s with the 1802 Theatre Royal in the centre of the picture.

Public House and Market Tavern known as the Spread Eagle Hotel'. Included in the same sale were three cottages at the rear of the hotel in Chapel Yard, accessible through the passageway, which were also included in the sale from Lune Street. It was bought by Mr Smith, the hatter of Market Place in Preston, for £3,410.

THEATRE HOTEL, Fishergate (1805–1987)

Presumably this hotel, often referred to as the Theatre Tavern, was built as a direct response to the erection of the Theatre Royal in the Guild year of 1802. They stood on opposite corners of Theatre Street, with my first record for the tavern being three years after the opening of the theatre, although it could have been there slightly earlier.

The Theatre Hotel did what most taverns did in similar circumstances, refreshing the theatregoers before and after the entertainment, and presumably those responsible for the entertainment also. I have even found evidence of backstage staff seeking refreshment during the performances. The original building also operated as a Commercial Hotel, the evidence for which gave me my earliest reference to the establishment – the *Lancaster Gazette* ran a story in February 1805 describing how a lodger threw himself through a top floor window, thereby paralysing himself.

The Theatre Royal continued well into the twentieth century, and when it was replaced by the ABC Cinema, the Theatre Hotel continued to provide the same service to cinemagoers and many others.

VICTORIA AND STATION HOTEL, Fishergate (1838–present)

These premises have seen several name changes, but they seem to have always been a combination of the words 'Victoria', 'Station', 'Royal', and 'Railway', with the exception of when it was called the 'Duck Inn Hotel'. It is now part of a small group, operated by a local company in the name 'Old Vic'. When it was first advertised to let in 1838, it was described as the 'Victoria Hotel'. The first tenant was a man called Charles F. Worthington, who moved from the Albion Hotel on Church Street. From 1841, for a period of thirty-six years, it was managed by Edward Croft, a surname that recurs through the first three-quarters of the nineteenth century's hotel, as well as other trades. For example, Crofts have been involved in the newspaper industry and the building industry for much of the last 200 years, with the latter still represented in the construction of top quality conservatories and orangeries in the greater Preston area. They are all believed to be the same extended family. See also, the Continental Hotel on page 35.

It first opened due to the arrival of the railway in Preston, and for the greater part of its life it benefited greatly from the railway's existence. In addition, it was a favourite banqueting and function venue for weddings and other celebrations, but today it is non-residential and operates as a public bar. In its early days, it would have experienced a lot of local competition, but at least six of those competitors were swept away in the 1870s, when the need to widen the railway lines and the bridge over them became necessary.

While second-rate entertainers sought accommodation at less expensive hotels and lodging houses, the stars would often choose this hotel while appearing at the Theatre Royal or the Corn Exchange; such was the case with Mdlle Christine Nillson, the prima donna Italian opera singer from Covent Garden, when she appeared here in 1869.

The bar inside the Old Vic.

An order was sent to Miles Doughty in London, requesting him to send, by the first passenger train, two of the largest boxes (11s each) of voice lozenges to Mdlle Nillson at the Victoria Hotel. They were duly delivered.

WAGGON AND HORSES, Lord Street (1796–present)

The Waggon and Horses has had several names during its existence. It currently trades as the Tithebarn Hotel but has, over the last ten years, been somewhat neglected by its owners due to the uncertainty of what was called the Tithebarn Project, a scheme that was intended to reinvigorate a part of Preston that had become a little run down because of the development of other areas. Indeed, the project would probably have seen the demolition of these premises. The project collapsed, and again there is an element of uncertainty about its future. In the eighteenth and early nineteenth century, the Waggon and Horses traded under the names of the 'Setting Dog', 'The Stocking', and 'The Volunteer'. However, for the greater part of its life it was known as the Waggon and Horses because of its close proximity to a number of noisy smithies from whose premises the beating of hot metal rung out.

In the late nineteenth and early twentieth centuries, the Waggon and Horses would have been instrumental in providing refreshments for visitors to the neighbouring Gaiety Theatre and Prince's Theatre. From 1858, when a large room suitable for balls and other entertainment was added to the inn, it began to offer entertainment in its own right. At its opening, 140 people sat down for a meal in the room. There followed, for several years, music hall entertainment similar to that being offered in several other taverns in the town. The entertainment at the Waggon and Horses was advertised as 'National Music Hall', in the form of ballad singers and serio-comic vocalists, accompanied by piano, violin and flute.

In 1861, the landlord notified the public that he had redecorated the new hall and purchased a new organ on which there would be played, every Sunday evening, a variety of sacred music, commencing at 6.30 p.m. In complete contrast, in 1867, the landlady, Anne Charnley, was summoned for breaching the One o'Clock Closing Act. The court was told that at 1.30 a.m., the police had visited her house and found 300 people assembled in the large room upstairs. Drink of all descriptions was on the tables, a band was playing and dancing was going on. The son of the licensee was told to put a stop to the proceedings, so he ordered the band to play the National Anthem, and the police left. They returned two hours later to find most of the company still there, and carrying on as before. She was fined 10s (50p).

WEAVERS' ARMS, King Street (now Manchester Road) (1805–1960s)

A most unlikely introduction to this tavern was from the *Lancaster Gazette* of September 1805, when a marriage notice appeared giving the details 'the pair William Heywood of Leyland, and Margaret Taylor, late of Walton-le-dale, were determined to have their courtship as brief as possible. The bridegroom accidentally went into the Weavers' Arms, Preston, and while drinking a glass of ale, the young woman unexpectedly came in, and seating herself opposite, a conversation took place, which in an hour ended in concluding the match.'

Despite being in an area that had a high density of inns, taverns and beerhouses, the Weavers' Arms was a busy place, offering accommodation to all manner of associations, many of which had a Catholic connection, who took advantage of the large, first-floor clubroom, capable of seating 150 people. Despite briefly losing its licence in 1863 following a complaint against the 'Dancing Room' – undoubtedly the clubroom – the Weavers continued to serve the Avenham and Frenchwood areas for a further 100 years.

WHITE LION, Syke Hill (1808–c. 1960)

The White Lion could be significantly older than we currently realise, because this area of Preston, at the foot of Stoneygate, is an ancient part of the city. Places such as the Hare and Hounds and the Old Pump Inn, which stood in Scotch Fields at the head of Albert Street – reputed to be the battle ground of the English and the Scots in Jacobite days – were both said to be in this restricted area, and could well have occupied the same site. The first reference, in 1808, has only come to light because of the death of the landlord's wife in that year, but how long he'd been there isn't known.

The involvement of a landlord in gambling, so prevalent in the 1800s, was shown in a notice in the newspaper *The Era* in March 1850 when, with regard to an event at the these premises, it announced that 'Old Joe of Preston, will run the Flying Clogger, also of Preston, the same distance as before, for £50 at Belle Vue. Money ready at Henry Rich's, White Lion, Preston.' Henry Rich's propensity for gambling was evidenced in his purchase of a racehorse called Odd Trick. He bought it at the York bloodstock sales for 52 guineas in 1855, and two years later, following four winning performances, sold it for £1,400.

Left: The Weavers Arms.

Below: The White Lion.

Chapter Three

West of Lancaster Road

For the area outside Ringway and London Road, I intend dividing the remaining area into two portions. For that purpose I will use Lancaster Road, a portion of North Road, and Garstang Road as the dividing line, with those public houses on the west side of those roads out to the city boundary being covered in chapter three, and those east to the River Ribble, in chapter four. The northern limit of the old borough can be regarded as Blackpool Road, from its eastern point at New Hall Lane to its western extreme in Ashton.

There are three public houses outside of that general guide, with the Cattle Market Hotel in this chapter, the Bowling Green Inn on Ribbleton Avenue, and the Fulwood Railway Hotel on Longridge Road at the Gammull Lane junction.

ADELPHI HOTEL, Fylde Street (1838–present)

The Adelphi Hotel is as close to the epicentre of Preston's transitory student population as it is possible to get, and it takes full advantage of the opportunities that affords.

In the early part of the nineteenth century, another tavern stood on the spot where the Adelphi is now, before Adelphi Street was constructed. The name of that public house was the Fighting Cocks. It was demolished in 1837 and replaced with a new one, on the same spot but in a manner that permitted the construction of Adelphi Street, after which the new hotel took its name.

In the months leading up to the construction of Friargate and the new hotel, serious election riots at the Fighting Cocks probably contributed to the change of name; the many column inches of graphic reports identifying where the trouble was centred will have done little for its reputation.

It is worth noting that despite its being close to Canal Street, now Kendal Street, and its former population of mainly immigrant Irish millworkers, whose propensity for fighting seemed to have been insatiable, almost no trouble at all was reported from the Adelphi Hotel – a sign of firm management. Others in the area weren't so fortunate.

Above: The Adelphi Hotel. *Below:* The Cattle Market Hotel.

CATTLE MARKET HOTEL, Brook Street (1867–present)

Known colloquially as 'The Big House', this impressive building was constructed by the Corporation in 1867, with the simultaneous construction of a new market for the trading of livestock. A slaughterhouse was included in the plans for it. The site was chosen for its proximity to the railway lines, for it had been recognised that the railway was a growing contributor to the prosperity of Preston.

It was anticipated that the market would attract farmers and dealers from a wide area, and so it proved. The hotel had nine separate cellars, all 15 feet in height, each of which held different products, as well as a first-floor dining room almost 50 feet in length. There were in excess of 100 people at the dinner to celebrate the opening of the hotel, a combination of meat trade representatives and the Corporation. It also offered ten bedrooms and stabling for thirty-two horses, the property of both residents and day visitors.

The market operated successfully for well over 125 years, and was so busy that the 9-acre site was a 'beat' in its own right during the days of the Preston Borough Police, with a constable on duty whenever the market was open. His office was on the opposite side of the entrance gate from the hotel.

Other premises sprang up around the time of the opening of the cattle market. In fact, a tavern that later became known as the New Cattle Market Inn was opened two years before the one at the cattle market. The market had been the subject of discussion for several years, and an entrepreneur spotted the opportunity and built this one 200 metres distant from it. Two years after the opening of the market, the Butchers' and Commercial Hotel was built at the corner of Brook Street and what is now Blackpool Road.

Both of these competitors are now gone, but the 'Big House' continues to operate. However, the non-public part of the building is now sadly underused, with only a portion of the property being used as living quarters for the licensee. In 2014, after an extensive refurbishment, the name of the house was changed to the Brook Tavern.

DOCTOR SYNTAX, Fylde Road (1838–c. 2006)

There were two taverns in Preston to carry this name. The first was in Molyneux Square, now a part of Lancaster Road, close to the Guild Hall. They were both named after a racehorse that won the Preston Gold Cup on seven occasions, as well as five Gold Cups at both Lancaster and Richmond. The prize value in each race was 100 guineas.

When the Molyneux Square tavern closed around 1840, the Fylde Road one opened, with its first licensee being William Bond, a stonemason by trade. He went on to make a fortune from importing and exporting through Liverpool and Preston ports. He was also to build the Port Admiral Hotel on Lancaster Road, rich with stone carvings.

The Doctor Syntax closed its door in around 2006, but has reopened as a Chinese restaurant, which has gained a reputation for quality.

DOG AND PARTRIDGE, Friargate (c. 1772–present)

The date over the entrance tells us that this inn dates as far back as 1772, but it is claimed that it played its part in the Rebellions of 1715 in terms of supplying the

The wall of shields and insignias at the Dog & Partridge.

troops with victuals and other supplies. The notice presented to the landlord read, 'Sir, Give the bearer instantly ten bushels of Oates and Goodly Victuals, for the use of Cavalry quartered at the Barr, under paine of Military Execution, BY ORDER OF THE COMPANY OF FORAGE'. There was possibly an inn of the same name, on the same or similar spot before the present building.

In the 1840s, there must have been far more space at the rear of the inn, for they often held wrestling tournaments for up to thirty-two contestants, attracting entrants from Cumbria and other areas of similar distance, along with large crowds to both watch the sport and gamble on the outcomes.

During the final decades of the twentieth century, the Dog and Partridge attracted several diverse groups of customers, from former service personnel, as evidenced from their marvellous collection of regimental insignias, to motorcycle enthusiasts, who for some years gathered here to discuss and otherwise enjoy their passion.

For the past thirty years, the Dog and Partridge has been fortunate to be run by one of the trade's leading licensees, a man who has also played a significant role in the Licensed Victualler's Association in Preston, Ronald (Ronnie) Fitzpatrick.

DUKE OF YORK INN, Friargate (1825–c. 2011)
Firmly rooted in the first quarter of the nineteenth century, this inn seems to have experienced difficult times due to the heavy presence of Irish immigrant millworkers,

who lived close by in the Canal Street area, but also good times in the hands of the Noblett and other families. Part of the Noblett family was connected by marriage to the Noble family of brewers, maltsters and innkeepers, and together they played a significant part in Preston's licensed past.

From the mid-1850s, a wholesale business grew out of the premises, and succeeding landlords continued to trade in this manner. The Noblett family also had the advantage of controlling two other public houses at the same time – the Horse Shoe in Church Street, and the Sawyers Arms and Plumpton Brook Inn, an awkwardly named tavern that had two entrances, one from Snow Hill, and the other in Lawson Street. Presumably they were once two taverns, but there is no evidence to support that theory.

The Duke of York traded strongly throughout the twentieth century, later becoming a recipient of the trade brought by UCLan, but it has now been redeveloped as a restaurant with a growing reputation.

GENERAL HAVELOCK HOTEL, Plungington Road (1860–2007)
General Havelock, who was mainly associated with battles in India, has lain in a tomb in Lucknow, India, since his death in 1857. He possibly lay a little less easily after this inn adopted his name in 1860, for he was a staunch teetotaller. Havelock Street, on whose corner the inn stands, was named by Messrs Joseph Harrison & Son of Galligreaves Mill, who had constructed the street in connection with their business in the year of Havelock's death, so the inn was probably named in consequence of that.

The inn stands in the middle of what was the Moor Hall estate, and was part of the outward development of Preston through the nineteenth century, first with Adelphi Street, and later its continuation, Plungington Road. Throughout the twentieth century, the Havelock played its part in the social aspects of life in the Plungington area, but the gradual disappearance of small, private businesses over the years took its toll on the licensed houses as well, with only one out of the four Plungington Road beerhouses remaining – the Plungington Hotel.

GLOBE TAVERN, Corporation Street (1838–2010)
Although the Globe has a Corporation Street address, this only came about in the last twenty years of the nineteenth century. A previous building bearing the same name had stood on roughly the same foundations as the present building since before 1840. Its address, however, was in Heatley Street, on whose junction it now stands.

In 1900, eight years after the new building was completed, George 'Geordie' Drummond became the landlord. He had been an important member of the Preston North End Old Invincibles of 1888/89, and had run public houses in Preston both before and after this one. For much of that time he was also the trainer for the town's famous team.

The replacement building was certainly intended to make an impression on the public, and although it is now a Chinese restaurant, the building continues to retain its attractiveness.

GRAND JUNCTION HOTEL, Watery Lane (1866–present)
This house was built by its first landlord George Booth in 1866, and operated as a

The Grand Junction Hotel.

beerhouse. However, after just six weeks, he applied for a full licence on the grounds that many domestic properties were being built in the vicinity, and about 1,500 men were employed at the neighbouring Waggon Works, shipbuilding yards, and the quays along the River Ribble.

As time passed, industry changed and grew, and the Port of Preston was developed between 1884 and 1892 by rerouting the river and constructing one of the largest single docks in Europe, thereby opening up trade to the world. The Dock Estate workers and foreign seamen (to say nothing of the huge English Electric Company workers on Strand Road) contributed significantly to the Grand Junction's success.

The Grand Junction remained in the same family for at least forty-one years, passing to George Booth's son, John, around 1874. Today, it continues to trade alongside its neighbour, the Wheatsheaf Hotel, mainly serving the resident population of the Tulketh area. The Port of Preston is no more, and gone also are the massed workers of yesterday.

HOOP AND CROWN, Friargate (pre-1786–1936)

This was an interesting tavern that stood immediately to the north of the Hippodrome on Friargate, and closed just before the Second World War. A typing error took my knowledge of these premises back a further forty years, for the name of the place had been written as 'Hoop and Grown'. Putting 'Hoop Preston' into the search engine of the Lancashire Record Office produced a legal document that referred to a different building on the same spot, many years earlier. It even recorded the fact that for a short period its use had been as a domestic residence only.

During the nineteenth century, the most notable landlord was Edmund Barry, a Londoner, who ran the place for several years with his sisters. He frequently wrote his own poetry, which he paid to have published in the local papers, extolling the virtues of his tavern and 'Barry's Home-brewed Nut Brown Ale'. He employed unusual marketing strategies, such as spreading the rumour through all town centre public houses that he had 'hanged himself behind the bar of the Hoop and Crown', motivating visitors to flock to the place to witness the deed.

Edmund Barry was the landlord for only five years from 1869 to 1874, but his sister, Kate, continued after his untimely death, and remained there for another fourteen years before marrying James Hall, who took the licence over from her.

A story that has been passed down through the family who ran the Hoop and Crown from 1901 to 1913 related to a man in a 'plod' cap, believed to be a type of plaid. It is said that while drinking on the premises, he kept his horse and cart in the stable yard at the back. He was abusive and cruel towards the horse, which eventually provoked the animal into kicking and killing him. They claimed that the ghost of the man was seen a number of times before the inn closed for the final time, and years later, after C&A Stores had taken over the property, staff reported that they thought the place was haunted, and that there was an 'icy chill' in the stock rooms. They are exactly where the stable yard was.

LAMB AND PACKET INN, Friargate (1807–present)

Standing as it does at the corner of Friargate and Kendal Street, one could be excused for thinking that this hotel must have had a poor reputation in the nineteenth century. Kendal Street was once known as Canal Street, a thoroughfare that extended as far as the Preston to Lancaster Canal. It was one of the most deprived areas in Preston, with many of the neighbouring public houses suffering outbreaks of violence, and although there were isolated incidents at the Lamb and Packet, they suffered far less.

Prior to 1876, the premises stood 15 feet further forwards into the middle of Friargate. In that year, the Corporation requested the taking down, setting back, and rebuilding of the hotel in order to widen the road and extend the footpath. The rebuilt hotel must have been considerably larger than the original one, for the following year a question was asked in council with regards to the rebuilding of another public house, when the comment was made 'that it was hoped that if such a house be contemplated it would not be of such contemptible proportions as the Lamb and Packet'.

Like its close neighbour, the Adelphi Hotel, it stands in the midst of the student quarter of Preston, but is somewhat different in character to that place. It is a clean, open-plan, welcoming, food-offering inn with a good reputation.

LANE ENDS HOTEL, Blackpool Road (1855–present)

In an advertisement in June 1855, this property was described as 'suitable for an inn'. It boasted stables, a shippon, a coach house, a brewhouse and a granary, and further land was available that was suitable for a bowling green; an inn with a bowling green it

The bar at the Lamb and Packet Inn.

A very early photograph of the Lime Kiln Inn taken in the 1800s.

became. Ashton was described at this time as a hamlet and the address was Long Lane rather than Blackpool Road. Even as late as 1890, when the hotel was again advertised to be let, it still had shippons for fifty cows, piggeries, and it was still brewing its own beers. The proximity of the Preston to Kendal Canal (and the New Cattle Market on Brook Street from 1867) will have been particularly convenient to the hotel in its farming days.

The crossroads at Lane Ends, Ashton, has always been an important one, and now it is also a busy one. The hotel has expanded during the last fifteen years, incorporating neighbouring property on Blackpool Road, and changing what was predominantly a working man's beer-drinking resort, into a multipurpose, food-serving establishment for their enlarged range of customers and families.

From the late 1960s until the time of its redevelopment, the Lane Ends Hotel achieved almost cult status as a Boddington beer drinker's mecca, and it remained largely trouble free.

LIME KILN INN, Aqueduct Street (1839–c. 2006)

In its last 100 years of existence, the Lime Kiln was noticeable by its red-and-white tiled frontage. It wasn't unique in this respect, even in Preston, for there were a number of other public houses similarly adorned, e.g. The Drovers' Arms and the Princess Alice Inn. It was, at one time, a tradition to paint a pattern of red-and-white squares on the doorposts of every public house, much like a chessboard. It was an ancient symbol that extended as far back as the Roman Empire, although its actual meaning has never been ascertained. It may simply have been a notice that was understood by even the illiterate, from a time even earlier than the more recognised inn sign.

The significance of the name of this inn can be found in the fact that directly across the road were a number of limekilns that owed their existence to the presence of the Preston to Kendal Canal, which was just yards away. Limestone would be conveyed from the north of the county and South Cumbria, and coal and other commodities would be taken in the opposite direction. This stretch of the canal no longer exists, and neither does the extremely narrow bridge over which the canal was carried.

In 1875, a large explosion occurred at the Lime Kiln Inn. Windows were blown out of the house, which quickly filled with smoke. It was the result of a disagreement between the landlord and a customer who didn't believe that a container behind the bar held gunpowder. The friend, still doubtful, threw some onto an open fire. When the landlord, James Ridge, was charged, he said, 'I know nowt about it. Fetch Kay in.' When William Kay came in, he admitted putting the gunpowder on the fire, and Ridge asked, 'Do I know about it?' Kay replied, 'Thou knows all about it; thou led me into it!'

The Lime Kiln Inn is now a Chinese restaurant.

MOOR PARK INN, Garstang Road (1837–present)

This was a Corporation-built public house that was intended to take advantage of the cattle market that stood across the road from it. There was still no English Martyrs' church, no St George's Road, and Aqueduct Street had still not been opened up to Garstang Road, the main road north.

The opening of this inn occurred a mere five years after the introduction of the Temperance Movement, and in council proceedings, Joseph Livesey, the founder and creator of the movement, said that he was sorry that the Corporation had built it, and should the new body continue to build these nests of crime, he should move that opposite each there should be built a Temperance Hotel. It didn't happen in this instance.

In 1845, Garstang Road was still a turnpike toll road, and in that year the tolls were let to the landlord here, Peter Greenough, for £1,207 for the year, a £2 increase on the previous year.

At one time, almost all inns, taverns, and beerhouses brewed their own ale on the premises, but the Moor Park Inn has the distinction of being the final one to do so in Preston. Jimmy Dougal, the former Preston North End and Scotland footballer, was the landlord at the time.

NEPTUNE HOTEL, Strand Road (1865–1990s)

When a full licence was granted to this Corporation-owned property in 1875, after operating as a beerhouse for ten years, it caused great consternation. The reason was that apart from another public house on the opposite corner of Marsh Lane, the New Quay Inn, there were no other houses for a considerable distance.

However, with the benefit of hindsight, the decision to grant it was an understandable one, for domestic housing was increasing considerably around these two sentries at the foot of Marsh Lane, and across from both these properties, the Port of Preston was

Neptune Hotel under repair in the early twentieth century.

growing in importance commercially, with a new dock development being mooted. As Preston grew, industries developed in the area, to a point where it was an extremely dynamic part of the town. Conversely, years later, as the English Electric Company of Strand Road and others moved out of the area, workforces were reduced. The introduction of the Ring Road in the 1960s eventually skirted the side of the Neptune Inn, and wiped out the New Quay Inn. The Neptune Hotel became totally isolated at an increasingly complex road junction, and it closed in the 1990s.

NEW BRITANNIA INN, Heatley Street (1841–present)

For a very brief period at the start of its life, this inn was called the 'John Bull', but by the time of the 1841 census it had already acquired the name it still holds. It stands very close to one of the main highways in Preston, Friargate, and yet has remained relatively anonymous, tucked 30 metres away from that highway.

That anonymity seems to have been the connecting thread throughout its existence, for despite this, it has been a well-run, thriving hostelry for about 175 years. During the twentieth century, it remained in the same family for over fifty years, from Thomas Noblett in 1925, to his brother-in-law, John McClarnan, and later to John's son, Edward. Eddie, as he was known, was a career landlord, who was well known for the condition in which he kept his beer, and the straightforward way he ran his business, employing only family.

Today, like most city-centre public houses, the small, character-filled rooms have been opened out to provide full vision for security cameras, but it maintains its ability to demand the close scrutiny and approval of the local CAMRA group. Its proximity to one of the new university buildings in Heatley Street has certainly raised its profile, and there seems no reason why it shouldn't have a bright future.

NEW SHIP INN, Watery Lane (1831–2011)

The use of the word 'old' or 'new' is relative to the subject in question, and its use here is against the existence of a 'Ship Inn' on Fylde Road, which preceded it by a couple of years. It may, of course, be older than that, but they're the dates that are available.

The original building's address was 'Marsh End', for that is what much of the area was – a marsh. The new Port of Preston was still sixty years away, and the few grand mansions that existed along that stretch of the River Ribble only required an approach that would accommodate a coach and four.

From its first day, the landlord of the New Ship Inn combined his interests with that of a smallholder, and this continued until around 1847, when at an auction on the premises there was a disposal of the whole of the farming stock, implements of husbandry, as well as the growing crops. In addition to two ponies, there were two breeding sows, two speaning (weaning) pigs, and eight sucking pigs.

Frequently, the extraordinary things that were produced on the smallholding in those early days came to the attention of the local press, such as the extraordinary bean (thought to be a broad bean), a plant that branched into four stems with thirty-five pods, which contained eighty-six beans weighing 7½ ounces. In the same year he produced 71 pounds of potatoes from three seeds. Several years later, a duck, owned by the same man, produced seventeen ducklings from the fourteen eggs she had been brooding.

From the 1890s, these premises benefited a great deal from the businesses on the new Dock Estate and Port of Preston, with vessels coming from the four corners of the world.

The replacement building for the original New Ship had a huge and well-used concert room that only ceased to function in the early years of this century. It is now a shisha café and smoking venue.

NEW WELCOME INN, Sizer Street North, Now Cambridge Street (1871–present)

Originally called the 'New Holly Inn', it only traded as such for a few months before changing its name. Its name would distinguish it from the similarly named 'Welcome Inn' on what is now Queen Street, but was there ever a 'Holly Inn' in Preston?

The compact nature of Victorian-era housing is typified with a trio of public houses off Aqueduct Street. Two of them still exist, this one at the corner of Ellen Street, and the Princess Alice, which lies barely 30 metres away at the corner of Hammond Street. It is difficult to imagine how Barlow Street and probably five or six terraced houses once separated them.

These inns have some common ground in that they both enjoyed lengthy tenancies with their respective landlords, particularly in their first 100 years. That's usually a sign of well-run, trouble-free establishments that attract little attention from the authorities, with the consequence that there is relatively little press coverage to affect that opinion.

ODDFELLOWS ARMS, No. 30 Adelphi Street (1841–c. 1970)

Just one of the nine public houses that have borne the name of the Oddfellows movement, with only this one, one on London Road, and the one on Park Road existing for any period of time.

While the Oddfellows Arms may not be the oldest inn on Adelphi Street, the vast majority of the fourteen different inns that appeared on that thoroughfare succeeded it, and there were countless others on the side streets off Adelphi Street.

It is of significant social interest that in 1871, the landlord, John Seed, his wife, Elizabeth, and their five children were living at a shop premises almost directly across the road at No. 107 Adelphi Street. The eldest daughter, just seventeen years of age, was the head of the household, with her sixteen-year-old brother assisting her in the shop. There were three younger children living with them aged eight, six and five years, who went to school.

(OLD) BLACK BULL INN, Friargate (1805–present)

There is a belief that there was a Black Bull on Friargate in 1776, and while it may have been on this spot, it is unlikely to have been the same building. My earliest record is from an auction held on the premises in November 1805, when the landlord was Richard Leach, so it must precede that date. There have also been two other Black Bulls in Preston. The one on Cheapside formed a part of the buildings that accompanied the

The New Welcome Inn.

The Oddfellows Arms.

Stan Eaton, the landlord of the Black Bull Inn.

pre-1855 town hall, and was presumably linked to the metallic remains on the Market Place itself, which were used to pinion the bulls during baiting events. The other one was on Church Street where Avenham Street now stands. The only date I have for that one was in 1732, when Henry Fleetwood owned it.

An acknowledgment of its longevity can be seen behind the bar of the inn, where a plaque explains that 'the Old Black Bull is famously situated on the site of an ancient tunnel leading to an old monastery; tunnels used as hiding places by Priests fleeing persecution'. Needless to say that this has been interpreted as 'the priests used the tunnels to access the Old Black Bull undetected!'

In an interesting auction notice in 1837, there was mention of the 'Old Black Bull' situated at the 'Brown Channel' on the south side of Friargate. A brown channel was an open gutter that stood close to the junction with Lune Street. Down it will have flowed all manner of effluent, all of which would be open to the senses. The mere thought of it, on what was one of Preston's major thoroughfares, gives a graphic impression of life at the time.

Just four years later, in 1841, a 'commodious' shooting gallery using rifles and pistol was opened here from ten in the morning until ten in the evening. The advertisement was dated November, so it is assumed that it was an indoor range.

The Black Bull continues to thrive, having had the benefit of almost fifty years under the strong management of three individual landlords. The current one has been mine host for a quarter of a century, is a keen supporter of CAMRA, and an active promoter of a huge range of real ales, running regular regional festivals and picking up a 'Pub of the Year' award in 2012.

OLD BRITANNIA TAVERN, Friargate (1807–c. 1962)

This small tavern, standing at the side of Lill's Court, has a further connection to that name. The Lill family owned the land on which the 'Old Brit' stands when it was bare, and John Lill, the pub's builder, was the first landlord. The small court of around a dozen cottages that stood in Lill's Court was said, at one time, to have quite a reputation. Few people saw behind the wooden door that obstructed the view from Friargate, but it is said that those who entered were confronted with the most marvellously maintained cottages, the tenants of which were so competitively house-proud that the sight of them was so incongruous with similarly situated cottages as to be almost beyond belief.

The history of the tavern has been woefully under-recorded, but that can be a positive indication that it has been well run and kept free of trouble. It is good to record that in 1874, James Isherwood, the landlord at the time, bequeathed £1,000 and £100 respectively to the Preston Royal Infirmary and the Blind Institute.

It is a little ironic that one of Preston's smaller taverns has been replaced on roughly the same site by another Wetherspoon's.

The Old Britannia Tavern.

OLD SIR SIMON, Friargate (1818–1907)

This pub was named after Sir Simon Fraser, 11th Lord Lovat, who was particularly famed for his violent feuding and dramatic changes of allegiance. In 1715, he had supported the House of Hanover, but by 1745 had changed his support towards the Stuart claim to the crown. He was among those highlanders who were defeated at the Battle of Culloden, tried for treason, and became the last man to be publicly beheaded on Tower Hill in London.

During much of the nineteenth century, the Old Sir Simon was under the control of the Mercer family, beginning some time before 1861 with James Mercer, before later passing through the hands of his wife and son, also James, until close to the end of the century.

After its closure in 1907, the premises served several purposes: as the Torella coffee bar, more recently as the Bello restaurant, and currently as a Tesco Express.

PRINCE ARTHUR HOTEL, Moor Lane (1851–2011)

An advertisement in the *Preston Chronicle* in February 1859 gave an extremely good description of its character. To the rear of the hotel there was a brewhouse that was at least equal in size to the hotel itself, with the advert reading 'with the brew-house and large room over the same, occupied as a school'. The hotel was at the corner of Victoria Street, and the brewhouse later became known as the Victoria Brewery, but whether the school continued isn't known. In 1865, the brewhouse became yet another example of brew tub accidents, in this instance with an inexperienced brewer. While ladling ale out of the brewing boiler, the brewer lost his balance and fell into it. He died four hours later.

In almost every case of this kind, there has been mention of a platform or walkway around the boiler, and invariably the victim 'leant forward and over-balanced'. A solution would surely have been obvious, but the tragedies kept recurring.

In a sale notice of 1876, the brewhouse is noted as having been converted into a stable, but by 1892, when it was sold again, it was reported that the hotel had been disposed of, together with the brewery, stables, coach house, and buildings attached thereto. It had been bought by David Bramley, who was said to have a number of retail grocery shops under his control at the time, and to be trading as a wholesaler as well.

After attempting to take advantage of the trade available from its proximity to the university campus, trading under the name 'University Tavern', it has now been converted into a takeaway food retailer, serving the same audience.

PRINCESS ALEXANDRA, A.K.A. TH'OLE I'TH WALL, Fylde Road (1869–c. 2000)

In later years, this tavern was better known as 'Th'ole in't Wall', but there have always been doubts as to where the name had its origins. Some think that it referred to a hole in the wall by the Lancaster Canal directly opposite, through which canal folk would pass to visit the pub. Others think it has something to do with the railway bridge by its side, with its huge, arched underpass for pedestrians. There are some who think that there was a hole in the gable end of the upper floor of the inn, through which train drivers could be handed a drink as they passed. The most credible explanation came from a descendent of a former landlord, who explained that there used to be a set of stone steps that led down from a hole in the wall and ran alongside the railway track, down to the pavement, enabling train drivers to access the place for a drink.

SHIP INN, Fylde Road (1829–present)

For an inn that has been in existence for such a long time, there is very little documented evidence available, and probably a sign that it has been well run. The first date I have for it is 1829, when Hannah Booth was the landlady, an unusual circumstance unless she'd been widowed after moving to the inn with her husband. If that were the case then it could possibly mean an earlier starting date.

There are several references to 'the large room' being used for political meetings, private functions, such as the anniversary dinner given by the Preston Branch of the Steam Engine Makers' Society in 1864, meetings of friendly societies such as the Oddfellows, and coroner's inquests.

There are many accounts of inquests that include factory and mill accidents, a man being burnt to death in his bed, cases of drowning in both the nearby canal and the more distant River Ribble, a child that fell into a dolly tub (wash tub) full of boiling water, and the landlord of the nearby Junction Inn, who fell into the mash tun of boiling water while brewing ale at his inn.

Today, the Ship Inn is known as the 'Ship and Giggles', and is the haunt of predominantly university students, being situated immediately next door to the original and main part of UCLan, although it is now completely surrounded by numerous additions to the university complex.

SUN INN, Friargate (1808–present)

There have been at least three 'Sun' public houses in Preston, a fact that can have confusing consequences, but only this one's name remains. While the earliest date I have for it is 1808, I am convinced that either this, or a predecessor with the same name, stood on this site when the Town Barrs were situated almost at its door in the eighteenth century during the periods of Jacobean fighting.

In the late 1830s, it was in the hands of James Hull. He and his two brothers were builders who were also involved in the licensed trade, and they later went on to set up a brewery in Glovers' Court, establishing their own portfolio of properties in much the same fashion, and in competition with, Matthew Brown's brewery.

The first sixty years of the twentieth century here were dominated by the Hacking family, who moved into the Sun in 1902. When Edward Hacking died in the early 1940s, control passed to his wife. Their son, Thomas, then took over the reins from her and remained until around 1960.

Today, the Sun Inn offers residential accommodation, and continues to trade in an area that is now dominated by the needs of the students of UCLan.

WHEATSHEAF HOTEL, Water Lane (1839–present)

The date that accompanies the Wheatsheaf motif above the roofline of this public house declares that it was built in 1892. It was rebuilt by the Corporation, who had owned

The Sun Inn, Friargate.

it since at least 1843 when it was advertised 'To Let', along with its outbuildings and gardens. There has undoubtedly been a Wheatsheaf Hotel on this spot since long before that date, and it is thought that in around 1824, it had been known as the 'Hesketh Arms', with the address Preston Quay. A wheatsheaf forms part of the heraldic sign of the Hesketh family, who used to live in the old Tulketh Hall, which dominated the high ground behind the Wheatsheaf Hotel and had fantastic views along the River Ribble towards the estuary. It has to be remembered that, at that time, the river will have taken the course of what we now know as Watery Lane, before the docks were created and the river course was altered.

During the earlier part of the nineteenth century, there was a 'pinfold' in the yard at the rear of the hotel, which was used to confine sheep or cattle found roaming, probably on the marsh opposite. The huge workforces employed by the Port of Preston and companies like English Electric are long gone, but the Wheatsheaf Hotel, and its close neighbour, the Grand Junction Hotel, still trade at the foot of Tulketh Road.

Chapter Four

East of Lancaster Road

ALBERT HOTEL, Ribbleton Lane (1851–1960s)

The Albert Hotel is said to be the first public house outside the centre of Preston to offer meals at lunchtime for predominantly millworkers. Although this happened at a much later date (early 1900s) the hotel had a reputation for its catering abilities. In August 1851, the millworkers from the mill of J. & H. Seed gathered on Ribbleton Moor for a sports day, where 'exciting trials of speed and strength' took place. There followed, in the new warehouse of that company, a 'most hospitable repast of good old English fare' for the whole of the 400-strong workforce, served up by Mr and Mrs Thomas Smith of the Prince Albert Hotel.

A sale advertisement from 1852 gave a good impression of the facilities at the Albert Hotel, which included a brewhouse and stables, and all necessary outbuildings, and 'commodious Skittle and Quoiting Grounds attached'. On the first floor was a clubroom capable of seating around 200 people, and on the second floor there was a further room, the same size as the clubroom, which could easily be converted into four bedrooms.

The view in the photograph only became possible when neighbouring properties were demolished in the early 1960s, giving a good idea of the overall floor space available.

BIRLEY ARMS, New Hall Lane (1853–1970s)

The Birley Arms was one of the many inns and taverns that sprang up on New Hall Lane during the time when 'New Preston' was growing around the huge Horrocks's mill factory on that thoroughfare. In the photograph, the premises had become isolated from the surrounding houses that had been demolished, but the converted coach entrance to the inn is still clearly discernible, evidence of busier times. Indeed, in an early sale notice, the Birley Arms were described as 'having good stabling and a lock-up coach house'.

In 1885, a dreadful fire occurred at these premises, completely gutting the building and destroying the contents. The landlord's eleven-year-old daughter was burnt to death. Harry Yorke, the proprietor of the Gaiety Theatre in Preston, presented a special performance of

The Albert Hotel.

The Birley Arms.

The County Arms.

a variety of entertainments in his theatre for the benefit of the family. Furthermore, Yorke had an additional interest in the event; one of the performers appearing at the Gaiety Theatre at the time, a man called Macolla, known as the left-handed Paganini, also lost all his possessions in the fire and, in leaping from the top floor of the house, broke both his ankles, rendering him a lifelong cripple.

COUNTY ARMS HOTEL, Deepdale Road (1828–2007)
Standing directly next to Preston Prison, it is said that the County Arms premises were used by visiting county court judges when they were on business at the town's courts.

For many years there was a huge bowling green to the rear of the hotel, where, apart from its intended use, wrestling matches were hosted, traditionally on Whit Tuesday. Up to forty-six competitors, the majority from as far away as West Cumbria, would assemble to compete for non-monetary prizes such as cups, silver snuff boxes, silver pencil cases and belts.

DEEPDALE HOTEL, St George's Road (1891–2013)
Standing in the shadow of the floodlights of the Deepdale home of Preston North End, this hotel profited from the home matches played by that team. It was, by a substantial distance, the closest public house to the ground.

Ironically, its existence only occurred because a licence request for a similar building on Deepdale Road was refused, and so the same builder erected this building. One of its earlier landlords was the former Preston North End goalkeeper, Peter McBride, during the years of the First World War.

As time has progressed, the Deepdale Hotel has found itself in the centre of a densely populated Asian community, and it is understood that, following its closure in 2013, it will be developed into an Islamic Centre. Coincidentally, an Islamic group has also acquired the building on Deepdale Road, opposite the Corporation bus terminus, which was intended as a hotel.

GREYHOUND INN, London Road (1836–2012)

In the Greyhound's early days, the landlord, Thomas Cooper, ran an additional business from the inn. He was a brickmaker by trade, and to the rear of the property were huge clay fields. He employed large numbers of men to dig the clay to make the bricks that were fired in ovens on the site.

Cooper's only predecessor at the inn, William Sergeant, left under a cloud after he had indecently assaulted the wife of another London Road landlord at the Cheetham Arms. He avoided prosecution by publishing a public submission acknowledging the offence, and begging the pardon of the lady and her husband.

November 1960 was important in two respects. In the first instance, a building fault resulted in the sudden collapse of the front face of the inn, and caused its eventual demolition and reconstruction. Until that date, if a licensed property was to retain its licence, it had to continue to serve the public during the period of reconstruction.

During the course of rebuilding, a customer who had called in for his regular pint was crushed and killed when an insufficiently propped wall collapsed on him. This incident was the catalyst for a change in the law, which then allowed licensed premises to close under such circumstances, without the threat of losing their licence.

The nature of London Road began to change shortly after the rebuilding, as large swathes of domestic property on the opposite side of London Road were condemned and demolished. However, the Greyhound Inn continued to trade until 2012, when it closed its doors for the final time.

HESKETH ARMS AND CEMETERY HOTEL,
New Hall Lane (1855–present)

The creation of the Municipal Cemetery either prompted or necessitated the construction of a hotel that would have the ability to offer catering and other facilities to parties of mourners, and the rather grand Hesketh Arms and Cemetery Hotel was the response. They were able to offer lock-up coach house facilities, and excellent stabling for horses, with dinners available at the shortest of notice. It had been built by Mrs Ann Seddon, who had vacated the 'Prince Albert Hotel', now known as 'The Sumners', in Fulwood, in order to accomplish it. The reason for its dual name isn't clear, but it's probable that it was to distinguish it from the Hesketh Arms on Lancaster Road at its junction with Walker Street.

In an article in the magazine *The Builder*, dated 14 December 1861, the author was looking at 'the black parts of Preston' when he wrote, 'At last, after passing a vacant plot with a board notifying that it is building land to let, we come to a group of ecclesiastical domestic buildings and the cemetery gates. We take the former to be the Superintendent's lodge, but we are mistaken. It is the "Hesketh Arms and Cemetery Hotel"! For a hotel

The Hesketh Arms.

to be so close to the lodge and entrance gates of a spacious cemetery of fifty acres, with three chapels in it, is an innovation for which we were not prepared.'

This article was published without the name of the author, and there is a school of thought that the writer was Charles Dickens, who had spent a period of time in Preston in the early 1850s, and later writing *Hard Times*. It is widely held that the fictitious Coketown in that novel was, in fact, Preston.

JERRY LOBBY INN, Salmon Street (1841–mid-1930s)

Perhaps previously known as the Engravers Arms, the façade of this former beerhouse still exists due to the interest and thoughtfulness of the owners of the property at the time. It is part of the complex that formed the company Liquid Plastics, and they made a conscious decision to retain this attractive frontage in their development work. The lettering and other embossed work beneath the upper windows were rendered over by a previous owner, but the man responsible for the maintenance work for Liquid Plastics was able to establish the original design, and formed new lettering and scrollwork from it.

It was said that the beerhouse took its name from the fact that there was a communal 'jerry' to the rear of the premises, and that in the nineteenth century folk would bring their bedpans for emptying. The lobby to it ran along the gable end of the Jerry Lobby.

MOORBROOK INN, North Road (1860–2013)

It would seem that five or six years before the closure of the cattle market that was

The New Hall Lane Tavern.

associated with the Unicorn Hotel, two new inns appeared adjacent to it. One was the Shepherds Inn at No. 372 North Road, and this one at No. 370, standing directly across the road from Moor Brook Mill. The Shepherds Inn closed in 1907, and its use changed to that of a retail shop. It was demolished in the 1960s.

In view of its reputation as one of the smallest public houses in Preston, it is difficult to imagine the scene when one reads a report such as the one in March 1863, when a meeting of forty of the Canary Fanciers' Society, with their wives and friends, 'sat down to an excellent supper'. It would appear that the landlord at the time, Joseph Banks, was a canary fancier, and there were reports of several canary shows being held there during his tenancy. There was a wide interest in keeping cage birds at the time, including those noted for their songs, such as the goldfinch and linnet.

In early 2014, the inn passed into the ownership of the company that run the Continental Hotel in Preston, and plans are in hand for its future. It is understood that the Moorbrook Inn will reopen by the end of May 2014.

NEW HALL LANE TAVERN, New Hall Lane (1865–c. 1980)

As the area known as 'New Preston' expanded, so did the number of public houses, and of those on New Hall Lane, with the exception of the Belle Vue Hotel, this was the last one to appear. For about four years it had been known as the 'Halfway House', a reflection of its approximate position on New Hall Lane.

From its first day the landlord was Robert Aspden, and he was still there after the name had been changed. However, just weeks later, he met his death when he fell into a cellar at the Mountain Stag beerhouse in Mill Bank, Church Street. The tavern changed hands shortly after this event, but by 1871, Aspden's son, also Robert, had returned as the licensee.

The tavern stood at the corner of Aspden Street, but whether there's a family connection to that name isn't known, though it is probable.

OLD ENGLAND HOTEL, Ribbleton Lane (1853–c. 2000)

Purpose-built in 1853 by James Walmsley, the first landlord was quick to let the public know of his intent. He was advertising his home-brewed ale at 4*d* a quart (that's 5 new pence for six pints), and informing them also that he had a four-stalled stable and a large, enclosed lock-up yard suitable for a conveyance, or for cattle and sheep, and further declaring to them that the Old England Inn 'is well situated as a baiting-house for persons going to or from Longridge, Chipping or Clitheroe'. 'Baiting' was a nineteenth-century word indicating the provision of food and rest for either people or horses.

The Old England enjoyed a long (although unremarkable) later life, standing as the most easterly public house on Ribbleton Lane, a busy arterial link into and out of Preston, and serving an increasingly populated part of the town. The next public house was the Bowling Green Hotel on Ribbleton Avenue, almost a mile further east.

OLD OAK INN, Ribbleton Lane (1839–c. 1960)

The first public house on Ribbleton Lane stood at the junction of St Mary's Street North, opposite the rear wall of Preston Prison. It was an impressive building with a coach entrance, but its history is woefully under-recorded, which is a shame, for the landlord who took over in 1840 published the following as an advertisement for his house and wares:

> Ho yes! Ho yes! Stout Englishmen all!
> Here's new to make you fain,
> That Brave old Knight, JOHN BARLEYCORN,
> Has risen in strength again.
> For many a year we mourned him slain,
> By means most dark and foul;
> But he lives, and defies his foes again,
> With his strong and flowing bowl.
> At the sign of the 'Oak', the brave old oak,
> In Ribbleton Lane, lives he,
> And all the world he asks to come
> That all who doubt may see.
> So come to the 'Oak', where CRITCHLEY plays
> Mine host, and fills each horn
> With double ale, the time to
> When rose Sir Barleycorn.

PORT ADMIRAL HOTEL, Lancaster Road (1854–1969)

The Port Admiral was one of the most memorable public houses in Preston, and its name was a cause of mystery, speculation and comment for over 100 years. The answer to the mystery has only come to light in the last few years, with the building and the name itself probably a memorial to the man who built it.

The man's name was William Bond, a native of Blackburn, who was a stonemason by trade, with his own yard and workforce. In 1841, he was the landlord of the Doctor Syntax on Fylde Road, where he had other stonemasons lodging with him. This would account for the plethora of stone engravings that adorned the Port Admiral building.

Throughout the 1840s and 1850s, he bought a number of ships and commenced business as an importer and exporter of all manner of goods, getting a real taste for the sea in the process. He was also involved with the construction of the Bonded Warehouse on Victoria Quay by the old Port of Preston. The combination of these facts gives us a clear motive behind his choice of name for the hotel.

When the hotel closed in the late 1960s, the statue of Lord Nelson, one of those on the roof of the Port Admiral, was taken by the brewery and displayed indoors at the Trafalgar Hotel in Nelson. The Trafalgar is now closed, and a man in Burnley is now believed to own the statue. The other two principal carvings were of Napoleon Bonaparte, which was sold at auction in 2013 in Yorkshire for around £2,000, and that of a Greek maiden, which some prefer to believe was an image of Lady Hamilton. She failed to sell at the same auction, and was most recently seen in 2014 in an architectural reclamation yard in Preston.

QUEEN ADELAIDE, New Hall Lane (1839–1990s)

With the exception of the first two years of its life, the Queen Adelaide was for almost fifty years run by the same family. For nearly forty years, the family Blackledge were the licence holders, but there followed James Helme and then Thomas Sim, who were both related to the Blackledges by marriage.

The catering facilities offered by the Queen Adelaide would, as was usually the case, be in a first-floor clubroom. In this case, there was a room that was capable of seating at least sixty people to dine at such an event. The 'Blooming Rose' Court of the Ancient Order of Foresters was often recorded as holding their dinners there, but they also held meetings of the Botanical Society, and one of the several natural history societies that came and went.

In the 1860s and early 1870s, there were meetings of the Preston Ancient Footpaths Association in the clubroom here, an organisation charged with investigating matters such as the loss of 'public' paths, such as the one that disappeared and became walled in following the Corporation's development of land on the Farington estate, which was made into a cemetery. However, at a meeting here in September 1871, it was revealed that two members of the committee who had been entrusted with the finances had misappropriated large amounts of money. It was decided to dissolve the association with the balance of the cash assets being donated to the Blind Institute – whether the embezzlement was the sole reason for the decision or not isn't known.

ROSEBUD HOTEL, London Road/New Hall Lane (pre-1841–1988)

At one time it was difficult to capture an image of this hotel without the inclusion of

The Rosebud Hotel.

one of the old circular, ornamental metal urinals that stood in the centre of the junction of New Hall Lane and London Road. Prior to its importance as a direct route to the Corporation cemetery at its furthest extent, New Hall Lane had been an important toll road to Blackburn, Clitheroe and other towns, and villages in East Lancashire and West Yorkshire.

Probably due to its conveniently accessed position, it became a common meeting place for traders, both legal and illegal. There are several interesting yarns about the exchange of partridges and other game birds by gamekeepers for goods less available in country areas. For those traders with a need to quantify their goods, they will have found the presence of a public weighing facility at the front of the property on London Road a distinct advantage.

During the second half of the nineteenth century, the Rosebud Hotel was an opportune base for carriers, with a Tuesday-only service to Withnell, and a six-days-a-week offering to Blackburn. The only serious brush with the law occurred in 1878 when, at the Brewster Sessions in September, the chief constable objected to the licence being renewed because of an incident at the hotel in May of that year when 'stones, bottles and other missiles were thrown from the windows of the house at police and military, with the landlord not taking proper measures to prevent it'. The licence was renewed, but the landlord left a short time after.

SHAWES ARMS, London Road (1837–present)

Formerly known as the Black Horse, this inn stands at the foot of Hudson's Brow, or London Road as it is known these days. It is situated immediately before the bridge

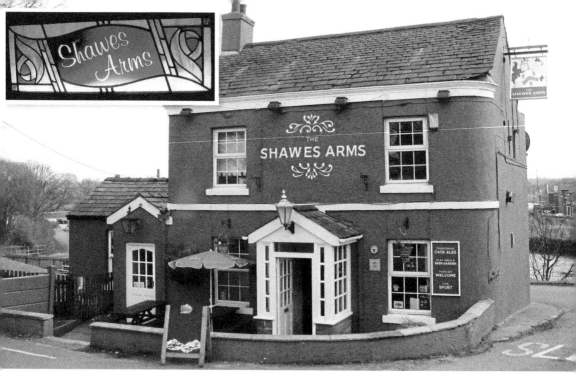

The Shawes Arms.

leading to Walton Flats, the low-lying area by the side of a particularly beautiful section of the River Ribble, and is an area steeped in the history of battles fought long ago, at a time when there was an even older bridge 100 yards downstream from the present one.

At the start of the twentieth century, the Shawes was still brewing its own ale and offering stabling facilities. Their offering of 'Special Accommodation for Cyclists' was undoubtedly an indication that the inn was conveniently placed for leisure cyclists, even at the early date of 1906.

A further indication of its convenient position on a major trunk road was the introduction of weekday lunchtime dining facilities in 'Captain Hook's Cocktail Bar, with the genuine ship's atmosphere'. Although the River Ribble is still tidal at this point, a deal of imagination would be required to capture a nautical experience from the Captain's bar!

In addition to this being the last licensed property on London Road as you travel south, it now has the dubious distinction of being the only licensed property on that road, which contrasts markedly with the record of anything up to a dozen such properties over the past 200 years.

SPINDLEMAKERS' ARMS, Lancaster Road (1849–1980s)

Although many public houses are named after a trade, the story in this particular case is fascinating. From the time it opened in 1849 until the end of the First World War, it was occupied almost entirely by the Dobson family. John Dobson had married his wife, Elizabeth, a native of Caton in the Lune Valley, in the mid-1840s, although she had been living in Preston for some time.

Information was received from a descendent of Elizabeth to the effect that her father was a spindlemaker in Caton, so while it was not unusual for an inn to adopt the name of the trade of its first landlord, I think it unlikely that many have celebrated the trade of a father-in-law from 25 miles away, but I see no reason to doubt that it was.

STONE COTTAGE INN, Egan Street (1853–2007)

Constructed of Longridge stone at the same time as the similarly constructed Fulwood Barracks, the inn was originally the residence of the commanding officer of the barracks. It carried a stone-engraved insignia high on the forward-facing gable end that was mirrored at the barracks, the building of which was completed in 1848. The insignia, or emblem, is a letter 'G' carved in the centre of two interlocking triangles, and stands for either 'Garrison' or 'Government'. It can therefore be assumed that it was occupied as a residence for about five years, and during that period it is believed it was known as 'The Cottage'.

It is said that the cellar was paved with old tombstones from nearby St Ignatius' graveyard, when part of it became the playground for St Ignatius' School. Perhaps that's the reason why the Stone Cottage gained a reputation as one of the most haunted public houses in Preston.

UNICORN HOTEL, North Road (1832–present)

Immediately to the north of this hotel stood the old cattle market, which ceased to trade in 1867 when business was transferred to the new cattle market on Brook Street. In its earlier days, and in keeping with its trading neighbour, the hotel was known as the 'Cattle Market Hotel' and later the 'Unicorn Inn and Cattle Market Hotel', and the majority of its trade was attracted by that source, with the large stone-built property offering accommodation to those requiring it.

The entrance to the yard of the hotel on the south of the property is still referred to as 'Cow Alley', although whether it played any part in the business of the market isn't known. There are to this day butcher's hooks on both the ground floor and in the cellars, which are reputed to have been storage for carcasses, but there is little direct evidence.

In 1876, at a time when several licensed premises were offering concert hall entertainment, a harmonic room was opened here to present a musical diversion on Saturday evenings, engaging a first-class pianist for the purpose. Live music and karaoke entertainment is still offered on more than one evening each week.

WILLIAM THE FOURTH, London Road (1832–2005)

King William IV was only crowned in 1831, so perhaps this inn had been known as something else prior to that. My first knowledge of it came from a 'To Let' notice in 1832, when it already appeared to be well set up for the purposes intended, with a brewhouse, a malthouse, a coach house and a three-stalled stable.

In July 1842, which was a Preston Guild year, there was a meeting here of a Court of the Ancient Order of Foresters, when, following a performance of an oratorio at the inn, there was a match of Royal Archery for prizes. It went on to announce that instruction in archery would be available there every Saturday between seven and nine in the evening.

Above: The Stone Cottage Inn. *Below:* The Unicorn Hotel.

Pub Index by Street

I have chosen to organise the index by street. In the majority of instances, all the inns in one street will be covered in the same chapter of the book. However, there are some exceptions to this, and in those instances, I have indicated after the name of the inn, in brackets, the chapter in which it should be included. The fact that there is an indication as to which area it is situated, does not necessarily indicate that there will be any editorial about it.

AVENHAM LANE (Chapter 2) – Anglers' Arms (1865–1904), Avenham Park Inn (1853–1990s), Fat Scott (1851–61), Foresters' Arms (1841–1905), Gas Tavern, or Gas Works Tavern (1825–41), Free Gardeners' Arms (1841), Frenchwood Tavern (1837–1990s), John O'Gaunt (1825–1950s), Palatine Hotel (1849–1980s), Prince Arthur Inn (1842–*c.* 1960), Rainbow Inn (1869–80), St John's Tavern (1861–1907).

AVENHAM ROAD (Chapter 2) – Thatched House (1857).

AVENHAM STREET (Chapter 1) – Duke of Windsor, formerly Garth's Arms (1826–*c.* 2000), Highland Laddie (1853–71).

BACK CANAL STREET, OFF CANAL STREET (Chapter 3) – Heart and Shamrock (1853–61), Olive Branch (1861).

BACK LANE, NOW MARKET STREET AND MARKET STREET WEST (Chapter 3) – except Angel Inn (1) (1838–present), Cock and Bottle, renamed the Derby Arms Inn (1) (1802), Farmers' Arms (1846–1980s), Farmers' Home (1851–53), Horse Shoe (1841), Prime Jug (1837–1907), Prince of Wales Feathers Inn (1843–1907), Wheatsheaf, synonymous with Prime Jug (1841), Whittle and Steel (1836), Woolpack Inn (1813–1924).

BACK WEIND, OFF TITHEBARN STREET (Chapter 2) – Green Man (pre-1798), Setting Dog, see Waggon and Horses (1711–36), The Stocking, see Waggon and Horses (1793–96), Waggon and Horses (1796–present).

BEDFORD STREET, OFF MOOR LANE (Chapter 3) – Duke of Wellington, a.k.a. Wellington Inn (1841–1910), Horrocks' Arms (1849–early 1920s).

BERRY STREET, OFF AVENHAM LANE (Chapter 2) – Bush Inn (1849–1950s).

BISHOPSGATE, OFF ORMSKIRK ROAD (Chapter 2) – Slaters' Arms (1851–69).

BISHOP'S PASSAGE, OFF TITHEBARN STREET (Chapter 2) – Carriers' Arms (1838–41).

BLACKPOOL ROAD, NEW HALL LANE TO LEA (Chapter 3) – Lane Ends Hotel (1855–present).

BLELOCK STREET, OFF MANCHESTER ROAD (Chapter 2) – The Saddle (1841–53).

BLUE ANCHOR COURT, FORMERLY OFF THE MARKET PLACE (Chapter 1) – Blue Anchor Inn (1790–1883).

BOLTON STREET WEST, OFF PITT STREET (Chapter 2) – Fox and Goose (1838–90).

BOWKER STREET, OFF OXFORD STREET (Chapter 2) – Oxford Tavern (1850–early 1930s).

BOW LANE, OFF FISHERGATE HILL (Chapter 2) – Buck i'th Vine (1838–*c.* 1963), Volunteer Inn (1855–1960s).

BOWRAM STREET, OFF MARSH LANE (Chapter 3) – Bull's Head Inn (1838–1910).

BRACKENBURY STREET (Chapter 3) – British Standard (1869–1980), New Park Inn (1869–1905).

BRIDGE LANE, NOW MARSH LANE (Chapter 3) – Bee Hive Inn (1825–1930), Elephant and Castle (1851–1910), Fleetwood Arms (1841–1930s), Free Gardeners Arms (1838–70), Mechanics Arms (1851), Queen Catharine (1841), Tacklers Arms (1861–64).

BRIDGE STREET, NOW MARSH LANE (Chapter 3) – Boat House (1838–41), Coopers Arms (1841–51), Hen and Chickens (1838–1902), Rose, Shamrock and Thistle (1861–93), Shovel and Broom (1832–35).

BRIERYFIELD ROAD, OFF WELLFIELD ROAD (Chapter 3) – Elephant, The (1868–1990s).

BROADGATE, OFF FISHERGATE HILL (Chapter 2) – Ribbleside Inn (1853–*c.* 2005).

BROUGHAM STREET, OFF ADELPHI STREET (Chapter 3) – Piel Castle (1859–1910), Victoria and Albert Hotel (1861–1907).

BROOKHOUSE STREET (Chapter 3) – Brookhouse Inn (1851–2000).

BROOK STREET, OFF FYLDE ROAD (Chapter 3) – Butchers' and Commercial Hotel (1869–1964), Cattle Market Hotel (1867–present), Cross Guns Inn (1853–69), Drovers' Arms (1868–c. 1979) George the Third (1853–1913), Hornby Castle (1856–2000s), Keystone Inn (1856–c. 1979), Lancashire Lasses (1859), Lancashire Leaper (1856), New Cattle Market Inn (1865–1990s), Star and Garter (1837–1960), Stockwell Inn (1854–c. 1965).

BRUNSWICK STREET (Chapter 4) – Brunswick Tavern (1853–1905).

BUSHELL STREET, OFF LANCASTER ROAD NORTH (Chapter 3) – Napoleon Inn (1851–1907).

BUTLER STREET, OFF FISHERGATE (Chapter 2) – Bush Inn (1851–71), Chorley Tavern (1862) probably erroneous, Commercial Inn (1851–74), East Lancashire Hotel (1857–c. 1876), Horrocks's Arms (1851–71), synonymous with Station Tavern, Queen's (Arms) Hotel (1856–1980s), Railway Hotel (1861–present) now Station Hotel, Stevenson's Arms (1851–75).

BUTLER'S COURT, OFF FISHERGATE (Chapter 2) – Elder's Beerhouse (1851–68), a.k.a. Bank Hotel Beerhouse

BYRON STREET, OFF MOOR LANE (Chapter 3) – Princess Royal Inn (1855–1960s).

CABLE STREET, OFF LOWER PITT STREET (Chapter 2) – Barley Mow (1825–1913).

CANAL STREET, NOW KENDAL STREET, OFF FRIARGATE (Chapter 3) – Highland Lass (pre-1840), Labourers' Arms (1841), Sir William Wallace (1838–c. 1870), Three Crown (1841–1907).

CANNON STREET, OFF FISHERGATE (Chapter 2) – Cannon Street Tavern (1866–1917).

CANUTE STREET, OFF KENT STREET (Chapter 4) – Brunswick Tavern (1861–1920s).

CARLISLE STREET, OFF POLE STREET (Chapter 2) – Bold Dragoon, renamed Guild Tavern (1838–1904), New Weavers' Arms (1861–1907).

CEMETERY ROAD, OFF GEOFFREY STREET (Chapter 4) – Cemetery Road Hotel (1881–c. 1999).

Chapel Walks, off Fishergate (Chapter 2) – Mattie's Whim (eighteenth century).

CHAPEL YARD, OFF FRIARGATE (Chapter 2) – Talbot Inn (1838–1930s).

CHEAPSIDE, OFF FISHERGATE (Chapter 1) – Black Bull Inn (1758–1861), Golden Lyon (1684).

CHURCH GATE, FORMER NAME OF CHURCH STREET (Chapter 1) – Red Lyon, a.k.a. White Lion (1732), Swan Inn (1732–78), White Lyon (1732–96).

CHURCH STREET (Chapter 1) – except Albion Hotel, a.k.a. Imperial Hotel, Royal Hotel, The Glass Barrel (2) (1832–1915), Bear's Paw, a.k.a. Grapes Inn (2) (1760–present), Black Bull (1732), Black Tiger (2)(1840–61), Blue Bell (2) (1716–present), Bull and Royal Hotel (pre-1670–present), Catterall's Beerhouse (1896–99), Church Gates, a.k.a. Eagle and Child (1832–39), Crown and Anchor (1824), Crown Hotel (1827–1913), Duke William (2) (1834–71), Flying Horse Inn (1729–32), George Hotel (2) (1924–90s), formerly the Horse Shoe Hotel, Grey Horse (1818–present), Harp Inn (4) (pre-1832–1967), Holy Lamb, renamed the Lamb Hotel (2) (pre-1818–2000), Jenny Lind (2) (1867–68), King's Arms Hotel (2) (1732–1898), New King's Arms (1898–present), King's Arms and Woolpack (1732), Old Dog Inn (2) (1715–present), Old Red Lion (1732–1827) renamed Crown Hotel, Oporto Wines Stores, see Crown Hotel (late 1800s), Queen's Hotel (1850–51), Red Lion Hotel (1809–present), Sir William Wallace, formerly Crown and Anchor (1825–29), Stanley

Arms (1827–52), Sun Inn (1732–78), Tap Room (1807–41), White Bull (1670–1791) became the
Bull and Royal Hotel, York Hotel, or York Tavern (2) (1839–1917).

CHURCH WEIND, OFF TITHEBARN STREET (Chapter 2) – Dog and Boson (late
eighteenth century).

CLAYTON'S COURT, OFF MARKET PLACE (Chapter 1) – Haymarket Tavern (1841–65).

CLAYTON STREET, OFF HUDSON STREET (Chapter 2) – Queen's Palace (1853–1960s).

CLOVER STREET, NOW ST ANNE'S ROAD, OFF ST GEORGE'S ROAD (Chapter 4) –
Charnock Hotel, formerly known as Clover Street Tavern (1870–present).

CORPORATION STREET, OFF FISHERGATE (Chapter 3) – North End Hotel (1888–1904).

CROFT STREET, OFF MARSH LANE (Chapter 3) – Fox and Duck (1849–1990s).

CROWN STREET, OFF LANCASTER ROAD (Chapter 3) – Crown and Shuttle (1852–1904),
Jolly Miller (pre-1840), Shuttle Tavern, synonymous with Crown and Shuttle (1852–1904).

DALE STREET, OFF STANLEY STREET (Chapter 2) – Amby Power (1859–83).

DEEPDALE ROAD (Chapter 4) – County Arms Hotel (1828–2007), Deepdale Bridge
Hotel (1857–87).

DEEPDALE MILL STREET, OFF RIBBLETON LANE (Chapter 4) – Duke of Edinburgh's
Hotel (1868–*c.* 1995).

DEEPDALE STREET, OFF DEEPDALE ROAD (Chapter 4) – Longridge Railway Tavern, a.k.a.
Preston and Longridge Railway Tavern (1841–1924).

DOVER STREET, OFF NORTH ROAD (Chapter 2) – Park Tavern (1838–1907).

DUKE STREET, OFF KING STREET, NOW MANCHESTER ROAD (Chapter 2) –
Fisherman's Cabin (1841), General Lee (1867–1960s).

DUKE STREET EAST, OFF LONDON ROAD (Chapter 2) – Welcome Inn (1852–*c.* 1960).

DUNDERDALE STREET, OFF MAUDLAND BANK (Chapter 3) – Junction Inn, later the
Preston Railwayman's Social Club (1869–*c.* 1930), West End Tavern (1851–*c.* 1960).

EAST CLIFF, OFF RIBBLESDALE PLACE (Chapter 2) – Park Hotel, a.k.a. New Railway Hotel
(1882–1950s).

EDGAR STREET, OFF NORTH ROAD (Chapter 2) – Black Fleet (1849), Sir Charles Napier
(1851–*c.* 1960).

EDMUND STREET, OFF PARK ROAD (Chapter 4) – Moulders' Arms, a.k.a. South Meadow
Street Tavern (1849–mid-1920s).

EDWARD STREET, OFF FRIARGATE (Chapter 3) – Ashcroft Arms (1835–99), Bowling Green
Inn (1815–89), New Duke (1841–84).

EGAN STREET, OFF MEADOW STREET (Chapter 4) – Coachmakers' Arms (1853–1901),
Prince Regent Tavern (1851–84), Stone Cottage Inn (1853–2007), Windsor Castle
(1838–1990s).

ELDON STREET, OFF BRACKENBURY ROAD (Chapter 3) – Eldon Hotel (1886–present).

ELIZABETH STREET, OFF LANCASTER ROAD (Chapter 3) – Rising Sun Inn (1847–94).

EUSTON STREET, OFF LADY PLACE (LADYMAN STREET) (Chapter 2) – Euston Hotel
(1869–*c.* 1965).

FISHERGATE (Chapter 2) – except Albert Hotel, a.k.a. North House (1851–1901), Alexandra
Hotel (1871–1980s), Borough Tavern (1) (1852–1917), Grey Horse and Seven Stars, formerly
the White Horse (1) (1732–*c.* 1923), Holy Lamb, later Borough Tavern (1) (1684), Mitre Inn
(1) (1790–*c.* 1950), New Legs of Man (1817–69), North Union (Railway) Hotel (1837–77),

GIN BOW ENTRY, OFF MARKET PLACE (Chapter 1) – Board, The (1825–29), Legs of Man (1818–29), Ram's Head Inn (1750–1881), Wheatsheaf (1804–81), White Hart (1805–82).

GLOVERS' COURT, OFF FISHERGATE (Chapter 1) – except Drummer's Return (1861), a.k.a. Glover Street Tavern (2) (1869–1904), Wellington Inn (1839–present).

GLOVER STREET, OFF AVENHAM LANE (Chapter 2) – Glover Street Tavern (1869–1904), Plasterers' Arms (1834–39).

GORDON STREET, OFF MOOR LANE (Chapter 3) – Gordon Street Tavern (1857–1904).

GORST STREET, OFF AVENHAM LANE (Chapter 2) – Oddfellows Arms (1859–61), Turf Tavern (1852–early 1930s).

GOULBOURNE STREET, OFF PEEL HALL STREET (Chapter 4) – Goulbourne Inn (1857–c. 1970).

GRADWELL STREET, OFF MARSH LANE (Chapter 3) – Soapery Tavern (1849–72).

GRAHAM STREET, OFF PEEL HALL STREET (Chapter 4) – Dover Castle (1869–1924).

GREAT AVENHAM STREET, OFF AVENHAM LANE (Chapter 2) – Avenham Tavern (1838–52).

GREAT GEORGE'S STREET, OFF NORTH ROAD (Chapter 4) – North Star (1841–1960s).

GREAT HANOVER STREET, OFF KENT STREET (Chapter 4) – Great Hanover Tavern, renamed the New Park Inn (1849–c. 1966).

GREEN STREET, PART OF WHAT IS NOW WALKER STREET (Chapter 3) – Crooked Billet (1832–41), Pet Dogs Inn (1858–95).

GRIMSHAW STREET, OFF CHURCH STREET (Chapter 2) – Clarence Hotel (1853–1917), former the St Leger, Dog and Pheasant (1841–2000s), Globe Inn (1853–1900), formerly Ropemakers' (1851–53), and Palace Inn (1861–65), St Leger Inn (1853–70), see Clarence Hotel.

GROVE STREET, OFF FYLDE ROAD (Chapter 3) – Aqueduct Inn (1842–1930s).

GUY'S ROW, OFF CHURCH STREET (Chapter 2) – Free Trade Inn, formerly Guy's Row Inn (1869–1907).

HAMMOND STREET, OFF GARSTANG ROAD (Chapter 3) – Duke of Cambridge (1869–1980), Moor Hall Inn (1861–c. 1979), Princess Alice Inn (1869–present).

HARRINGTON STREET, OFF MOOR LANE (Chapter 3) – Brewers' Arms (1851–86), later renamed Harrington Hotel (1886–1905), Field Marshall Lord Raglan's Inn, a.k.a. Lord Raglan Inn (1857–1960s).

HARRISON'S HILL, OFF MOOR LANE (Chapter 3) – Harrison's Hill Tavern (1840–c. 1969).

HAWKIN'S STREET, OFF ADELPHI STREET (Chapter 3) – North Star, a.k.a. North Street Inn (1853–c. 2002).

HEATLEY STREET, OFF FRIARGATE (Chapter 3) – Black Cat (1842–59), Globe Tavern (1838–2010), John Bull (1841), later renamed New Britannia Inn (1841–present), New Inn (1838–early 1930s), synonymous with Duchess of Lancaster, Ratcliffe Street, Pack Horse Inn (1841–1907), Pedestrian Arms (1869).

HIGGINSON STREET, OFF LANCASTER ROAD (Chapter 3) – Cock and Bottle (1841), Happy Cottage (1838–41).

HIGH STREET, OFF NORTH ROAD (Chapter 2) – Coach and Horses, a.k.a. Three Tuns (1796–1818), High Street Tavern (1871–95), Ormskirk Tavern, a.k.a. Judge and Struggle (1865–early 1930s), Painters Arms (1838–1960s), Prince of Wales Inn (1851–1907), Ring O'Bells (1834–68), Spotted Cow (1851–71), Vine Tavern (1851–1907), Vulcan's Arms (1841).

HOLSTEIN STREET, OFF MEADOW STREET (Chapter 4) – Stephenson's Arms (1869–*c*. 1990).

HOPE STREET, OFF FRIARGATE (Chapter 3) – Breton's Arms, a.k.a. Briton's Arms, British Arms, Hope Street Tavern, Paganini Inn, Whittle's Arms (1838–83).

HOPWOOD STREET (Chapter 4) Crystal Palace (1869–1907), Vine Inn (1851–1907).

HUDSON'S BROW, NOW LONDON ROAD (Chapter 2) – Garden's Inn, a.k.a. Strawberry Gardens (1853–78).

HUDSON STREET (Chapter 2) – Royal George Inn (1864–*c*. 1960).

JUTLAND STREET, OFF MEADOW STREET (Chapter 4) – Jutland Street Tavern (1867–1983).

KENT STREET, OFF GREAT GEORGE'S STREET (Chapter 4) – Duke of Kent (1850–2002), Duke of Sussex (1852–*c*. 1998).

KILSHAW STREET, OFF LANCASTER ROAD (Chapter 4) – Dog and Duck (1838), probably renamed Horse and Farrier (1851–1960s), Fox and Duck (1858), another name applied to the Horse and Farrier.

KING STREET, NOW PART OF MANCHESTER ROAD (Chapter 2) – Anchor of Hope (1856–57), Hunt's Arms (1832–41), King Street Tavern (1851–*c*. 2000), Lamb Tavern (1851–1904), Weavers' Arms (1805–1960s).

KNOWSLEY STREET, OFF AVENHAM LANE (Chapter 2) – Knowsley Hotel (1869).

LADYMAN STREET, OFF BOW LANE (Chapter 2) – Important Fact, a.k.a. Oddfellows Arms (1833–1910), Kendal Castle (1856–*c*. 2005).

LANCASTER ROAD NORTH, NOW LANCASTER ROAD (Chapter 3) – except British Queen (1849–1904), Builders' Arms (1868–1910), Cherry Tree Inn (1861–*c*. 1950s), Church House Tavern (4) (1849–1960s), Cotton Tree (1857), Griffin's Head (4) (1841–1907), Oddfellows Arms, a.k.a. Wakeley's Arms (4) (1837–51), Spindlemakers' Arms (4) (1849–1980s), Spinners' Arms (1866–1917).

LANCASTER ROAD SOUTH, NOW LANCASTER ROAD (Chapter 2) – Black-a-Moor's Head Hotel (1831–present), Boilermakers' Arms (1867–1917), Bull and Butcher(1804–81), Golden Cross Hotel (pre-1807–present), Green Dragon (1837–*c*. 1930), Hesketh Arms (1861–1901), Knowsley Hotel, a.k.a. Stanley Arms Hotel (1853–present), North Western Hotel, formerly Boilermakers' Arms (1867–1917), Port Admiral Hotel (1854–1969), Roebuck Hotel (1796–1902), Shoulder of Mutton (pre-1785–1881).

LARK HILL STREET, OFF LONDON ROAD (Chapter 2) – Sebastopol Inn (1855–*c*. 1960).

LAUREL STREET, OFF SHEPHERD STREET (Chapter 2) – Shepherds' Tavern (pre-1841–51).

LAWSON STREET, OFF HIGH STREET (now Ringway) (Chapter 3) – Bakers' Arms (1841–97), The Cotherstone (1843–44), a.k.a. Star Inn (1838–1960s), (New) Gas Inn (1854–1913).

LEEMING STREET, NOW PART OF MANCHESTER ROAD (Chapter 2) – Barton Arms (1867–70), The Falcon (1851–61), Lodge Bank Tavern (1841–73), Oddfellows' Arms (1851).

LIBRARY STREET, OFF ST JOHN'S PLACE (Chapter 2) – Guild Hall Tavern and Concert Hall (1866–1904).

LONDON ROAD (Chapter 2) – except Anchor Tavern (4) (1838–41), Cheetham Arms (1837–*c*. 1990), Chorley Tavern (pre-1845–51), Colliers' Arms (1841), Dog and Otter (1841), Greyhound Inn (4) (1836–2012), King William IV (4) (1832–2005), Oddfellows Arms (1861–1910), Prince Albert Tavern (4) (1851–1911), Rosebud Hotel (5) (pre-1841–1988), Shawe's

Arms (4) (1843–present), formerly the Black Horse (1824–43), White Boar (1851–*c.* 1960), William the Fourth (see King William IV).

LORD STREET, OFF LANCASTER ROAD, FORMERLY FROM TITHEBARN STREET TO ANCHOR WEIND (Chapter 2) – Derby Arms (*c.* 1894–1967), formerly the Joiners' Arms (1810–*c.* 1894), Grecian Inn (1851–95), Green Man (1798–1894), Imperial Hotel (1869–mid-1920s), Joiners' Arms, renamed Derby Arms (see above), Volunteer, The (1807), see Waggon and Horses (1796–present).

LOVAT ROAD, OFF GARSTANG ROAD (Chapter 4) – Lovat Road Hotel, formerly planned to be name St George's Hotel (1879–2005).

LUNE STREET, OFF FISHERGATE (Chapter 2) – Angel Inn (1838–present), Corporation Arms (1824–*c.* 1967), Exchange Tavern (1834), Market Tavern (1851–62), Spread Eagle Hotel (1807–1960s).

MAIN SPRIT WEIND, OFF FISHERGATE (Chapter 1) – Brewers' Arms (1838–41), Golden Ball Inn (1818–81), New Town Hall Tavern (1869–99), Sun Inn (1818–present), now trades as Revolution Bar.

MAITLAND STREET, OFF GEOFFREY STREET (Chapter 4) – Geoffrey Arms (1869–*c.* 1978).

MALT STREET, OFF DUKE STREET EAST (Chapter 2) – Brewery Field Tavern, formerly known as Lune Bridge Inn (1859–1904).

MANCHESTER ROAD, OFF CHURCH STREET (Chapter 2) – Balmoral Hotel (1891–1980s), formerly Black Swan (1827–91), Parkers' Arms (1869–1960s).

MARKET PLACE (Chapter 1) – Castle Hotel (1623–1905), Cross Keys Inn (*c.* 1684–1894), Mitre Inn (1684–1732).

MARKET STREET, OFF THE MARKET PLACE, FORMERLY, BACK LANE (Chapter 1) – except George Hotel (1898–*c.* 1926), Farmers' Arms (2) (1846–1980s) Market Inn (2) (1869–present).

MARSH LANE, OFF STRAND ROAD (Chapter 2) – except Boatman's Arms (1901–2006), Cart and Horses, formerly Carters' Arms (3) (1851–*c.* 1930), Dog and Duck (1850), Fly Boat Tavern (1851–57), Mariners' Home (1869–95), Marsh Lane Tavern (1869), Miners' Home (erroneous), see Mariners' Home, Navigation Inn (1851–*c.* 1930), New Anchor Inn, formerly called Twin Sisters (1852–1910), New Quay Inn (1841–*c.* 1960), Old Oak Tree (3) (1841–1990s), Sailors' Home, a.k.a. Sailors' Return (3) (1841–*c.* 1960), Spinners' Arms (1841), Springfield Inn (1834–1990s).

MASON STREET, OFF MEADOW STREET (Chapter 4) – Masons' Arms (1841–1950s).

MAUDLAND BANK, OFF FYLDE ROAD (Chapter 3) – Maudland Bank Inn (1856–*c.* 1967), Telegraph Inn (1869–*c.* 1960), Union Hotel (1850–*c.* 1960).

MAUDLAND ROAD, OFF FYLDE STREET (Chapter 3) – Bridge Inn (1828–*c.* 1930).

MEADOW STREET, OFF PARK ROAD, NOW RINGWAY (Chapter 4) – Army and Navy Hotel (1867–present), Clovers' Inn (1869–*c.* 1990), Meadow's Arms (1861–1990s), New Fleece Inn (1840–present), Royal Consort (1855–present).

MELBOURNE STREET, OFF UPPER WALKER STREET (Chapter 3) – New Baths Inn (1861–1910).

MILL BANK, OFF CHURCH STREET (Chapter 4) – Fortune of War (1841–early 1920s), Malt Kiln Tavern (1841–61), Mountain Stag (1861–69).

MILTON STREET, OFF MOOR LANE (Chapter 3) – Weavers' Arms (1859–70).

(1807–*c.* 1930).

OLD LANCASTER LANE, OFF AQUEDUCT STREET (Chapter 3) – Delhi Inn (1861–69).

ORMSKIRK ROAD, OFF LANCASTER ROAD SOUTH (Chapter 2) – Judge and Struggle,
a.k.a. Ormskirk Tavern (1865–early 1930s).

OXFORD STREET, OFF AVENHAM LANE (Chapter 2) – Fazackerley Arms (1846–1950s).

ORCHARD STREET, OFF FRIARGATE (Chapter 2) – California Inn (1853–61), Market
Tavern (1861–66), Plough Tavern (1851–1917), Travellers' Rest (1848–51).

PARADISE STREET, OFF MANCHESTER ROAD (Chapter 2) – New Hollins Inn (1841–1904).

PARK LANE, FORMER NAME FOR PART OF NORTH ROAD (Chapter 4) – Hunt's Tavern
(1841), probably synonymous with Machine Makers' Arms, North Road.

PARK PLACE, OFF NEW COCK YARD (Chapter 2) – Park Place Tavern (1867–69).

PARK ROAD, NOW RINGWAY, OFF CHURCH STREET (Chapter 4) – except Albion Hotel
(1904–50s) [formerly (New) Lamb Inn (1833–1904)], Durham Ox Inn (2) (1828–1968),
Free Gardeners' Arms (1838–39), Greyhound (1838–97), Guild Tavern, formerly the Bold
Dragoon (2) (1838–1904), Hornby Castle (1860), Oddfellows' Arms (1838–*c.* 1960), Park
Road Inn (1861–1962), Shooters' Arms (1841–*c.* 1963).

PATTEN STREET, OFF WALKER STREET (Chapter 3) – Church Tavern (1854), Duke of
Magenta (1868), Green Street Tavern (1859), Malt Shovel (1857), Ravenswood Castle
(1857), Shovel and Broom (pre-1840–1907), Soldiers Welcome (1859).

PEDDER STREET, OFF MAUDLAND BANK (Chapter 3) – Maudland Inn (1868–2005).

PEEL HALL STREET, OFF DEEPDALE ROAD (Chapter 4) – Lutwidge Arms (1859–*c.* 1930),
Peel Hall Hotel (1857–1970s).

PERCY STREET, OFF PARK ROAD (Chapter 2) – Coach and Horses (1838–1907).

PITT STREET, OFF FISHERGATE (Chapter 2) – Bay Horse (1831–99).

PLEASANT STREET, OFF AVENHAM LANE (Chapter 2) – Albert Inn, a.k.a. Prince Albert
(1840–1903).

PLUNGINGTON ROAD, EXTENSION OF ADELPHI STREET, NORTHWARDS
(Chapter 3) – General Havelock Hotel (1860–2007), Night Hawk Inn (1864), Oxheys Hotel
(1868–*c.* 1960), Plungington Tavern (1863–present), Royal Oak Inn (1865–*c.* 2006).

POLE STREET, OFF CHURCH STREET (Chapter 2) – Anglers' Inn (1839–1960s), Britannia
Inn (1841–42), Clock Face Tavern (1835), Contractors' Arms (1851–1904), Sir John Franklin
(1861–*c.* 1927).

PORTER STREET, OFF DEEPDALE ROAD (Chapter 4) – Hare and Hounds (1869–*c.* 1970).

POTTERY HILL, OFF BACK CANAL STREET (Chapter 3) – Daniel O'Connell (1869).

PRESTON QUAY, WATER LANE/WATERY LANE (Chapter 3) – Hesketh Arms (1824).

QUEEN STREET, OFF MANCHESTER ROAD (Chapter 2) – Druids' Arms (1841–95), Flying
Dutchman (1841–1904), Garden Gate (1825–72).

RATCLIFFE STREET, OFF HEATLEY STREET (Chapter 3) – Duchess of Kent, a.k.a. Duchess
of Lancaster and New Inn (1838–early 1930s), Pork Market Tavern, renamed Public Hall
Hotel (1869–*c.* 1950).

RIBBLE BRIDGE END, BOTTOM OF LONDON ROAD (Chapter 4) – Black Horse Inn
(1824–43), later became Shawe's Arms (1843–present).

RIBBLESIDE, OFF BROADGATE (Chapter 2) – Bowling Green Inn, formerly New Bridge Inn
(1837–1911), Little Bridge Inn (1837), Pleasure Boat Inn (1859–1910).

RIBBLETON AVENUE (Chapter 4) – Bowling Green Inn (1831–present), Fulwood and Railway Hotel (1865–present).

RIBBLETON LANE, (Chapter 4) – Albert Hotel, a.k.a. Prince Albert Hotel (1851–1960s), Anchor's Weighed Inn (1851–1960s), Birchall's Arms (1869–1960s), Bold Venture Hotel (1855–1960s), Derby Inn (1864–1980s), Foresters' Arms (1857–61), later the Third Duke of Lancaster's Own (1861–1960s), Fox and Grapes (1841–present), Guild Inn (1862–1960s), Nelsons Monument (1861–1904), New Sun (1853–1960s), Old England Hotel (1853–*c.* 2000), Old Oak (1839–*c.* 1960), Punch Tavern (1864–69), a.k.a. New Sun, Rose Inn (1861–1913), synonymous with Standard Rose Inn, Skeffington Arms (1856–2013), Star Hotel (1851–*c.* 1950).

RICHMOND STREET, OFF LONDON ROAD (Chapter 2) – Band of Hope (1854–61), became the Black Lion (1871–1940s), Lark Hill Tavern (1869–mid-1930s).

ROSE STREET, OFF SHEPHERD STREET (Chapter 2) – Rose Tavern (1864–69).

ST AUSTIN'S ROAD, OFF VAUXHALL ROAD (Chapter 2) – Morning Star (1869–*c.* 1960).

ST GEORGE'S ROAD, OFF GARSTANG ROAD (Chapter 3) – Deepdale Hotel (1891–2013).

ST JAMES STREET, OFF LONDON ROAD (Chapter 2) – Selborne Hotel (1895–1990s).

ST JOHN'S PLACE (Chapter 2) – Latham House (1858–95), Queen Adelaide, a.k.a. Queen Ann (pre-1838–mid-1930s).

ST JOHN STREET, OFF CHURCH STREET (Chapter 2) – Cross Axes Inn (1818–*c.* 1926), Fleece Inn, a.k.a. Golden Fleece Inn (1801–1907), Grapes and Punchbowl (1818–67), Hay Tavern (1841), Market Hotel (1857–*c.* 1960), Royal Oak (1808–98), Tim Bobbin (1840–42).

ST MARY STREET, OFF NEW HALL LANE (Chapter 4) – St Mary's Hotel (1851–*c.* 1990).

ST PAUL'S ROAD, OFF ST, PAUL'S SQUARE (Chapter 4) – Hyde Park Tavern (1856–1990s).

ST PAUL'S SQUARE, OFF PARK ROAD (Chapter 4) – British Standard (1849–1856), Edinburgh Castle (1838–2000s), Express Inn (1861–1891).

SALMON STREET, OFF LONDON ROAD (Chapter 4) – Anchor of Hope (1861), Engravers' Arms (1840–41), Jerry Lobby (1841–mid-1930s).

SALTER STREET, OFF NORTH ROAD (Chapter 4) – Old House at Home (1856–*c.* 1924).

SAUL STREET, OFF NORTH ROAD (Chapter 3) – Baths Hotel (1852–1967), New Cross, a.k.a. White Cross (pre-1839–94).

SAVOY STREET, OFF RIBBLE STREET (Lower Pitt Street) (Chapter 2) – Bull's Head (1838–95), Tom Bowling (1838–72).

SCOTLAND ROAD, FORMER NAME FOR PARK ROAD, OFF CHURCH STREET (Chapter 2) – Pied Bull (1824).

SHAMBLES, PART OF WHAT IS NOW LANCASTER ROAD, TOWN CENTRE (Chapter 2) – Golden Cross Hotel (pre-1807–61). Shoulder of Mutton (pre-1785–1881), see also Lancaster Road South.

SHEPHERD STREET, OFF STONEYGATE (Chapter 2) – Buck's Head (1841), Dog and Rat (1857–67), Forresters' Arms (1841–1851), Foundry Arms (1860–69), Liverpool House (1839–69), Oliver Cromwell (1839–69).

SIDNEY STREET EAST, OFF MOOR LANE (Chapter 3) – Ocean Monarch (1849–1900).

SIZER STREET, OFF BYRON STREET (Chapter 3) – Stone Jug Inn (1855–1907).

SIZER STREET NORTH, OFF AQUEDUCT STREET (Chapter 3) – New Holly Inn (1869), renamed New Welcome Inn (1871–present).

SNOW HILL, OFF BACK LANE (Chapter 3) – Plumpton Brook Inn and Sawyers' Arms (1826–1907).

SOUTHGATE, OFF NORTH ROAD (Chapter 4) – Drum and Monkey, a.k.a. Southgate Tavern (1855–1907).

SOUTH MEADOW LANE, OFF FISHERGATE HILL (Chapter 2) – Continental Hotel (1911–present), Cricketers' Arms (1864–2000s), South Meadow Tavern (1858–1976).

SPRING STREET, NOW PART OF BOW LANE (Chapter 2) – New Harbour Tavern (1869–1910).

STANLEY STREET, OFF EAST END OF CHURCH STREET (Chapter 2) – Jolly Sailors' (1838–51), King's Arms Hotel (1837–1990s), New Tiger (1859), Prince Consort (1863–1907), Stanley Street Tavern, a.k.a. Stanley Vaults (1843–1900), Three Crowns (1838–55).

STONEYGATE, OFF ST JOHN'S PLACE (Chapter 2) – Arkwright Arms (1851–92), St Leger Inn (1841–1904).

STRAIT SHAMBLES, RAN BETWEEN THE SHAMBLES AND THE MARKET PLACE (Chapter 1) – Shakespeare Tavern (1818–71), Swan with Two Necks (1803–81).

SYKE HILL, OFF STONEYGATE (Chapter 2) – Sir Tatton Sykes (1855–1904), White Lion (1808–c. 1960).

TAYLOR STREET, OFF FISHERGATE HILL (Chapter 2) – West End Tavern (1857–1990s).

TITHEBARN STREET, OFF LORD STREET (Chapter 2) – Barn Tavern, a.k.a. Tithebarn (Street) Tavern (1841–1917), Central Hotel (1926–c. 2000), Dover Castle (1841–44), Empire Hotel (1913–2012), Fruiterers' Arms (1865–1917), Guild Tavern (1926–c. 2000), Horse and Farrier (pre-1807–42), Lady of the Lake (1848–59).

TULKETH ROAD, OFF WATER LANE (Chapter 3) – Duke of Wellington, or Wellington Hotel (1869–present).

TURK'S HEAD YARD OR COURT, OFF CHURCH STREET (Chapter 1) – Gardener's Arms (1845), Man and Shoe (1838–49) Moulders' Arms (1857–70), Slip Inn (1863–77), synonymous with Turk's Head Inn (1802–1905).

TURNER STREET, OFF ST PAUL'S ROAD (Chapter 4) – Prince of Peace, formerly the Turners' Arms (1862–1913).

UPPER WALKER STREET, OFF NORTH ROAD (Chapter 4) – Pack Horse (1869–c. 1930), Raby's Arms (1845–c. 1861).

VAT STREET, OFF DUKE STREET EAST, NOW QUEEN STREET (Chapter 2) – Allies Inn (1853–1950s).

VAUXHALL ROAD, OFF SYKE HILL, AVENHAM (Chapter 2) – Vauxhall Tavern (1841–1904).

VICARAGE, THE, OFF BISHOPSGATE (Chapter 2) – Vicarage Inn (1841–53).

VICTORIA STREET, OFF MOOR LANE (Chapter 3) – Greenbank Tavern (1838–1966), Pioneer Inn (1853–1960s).

WALKER STREET, OFF WEST END OF FRIARGATE, (Chapter 3) – Victoria Tavern (1850–1907).

WARWICK STREET, OFF MOOR LANE (Chapter 3) – Royal Rover Inn, a.k.a. Royal Sovereign (1851–1902).

WATER LANE, OFF FYLDE ROAD (Chapter 3) – Fountain Inn (1861–1970s), Wheatsheaf Hotel (1839–present).

WATERY LANE, EXTENSION OF WATER LANE, WESTWARDS (Chapter 3) – Grand Junction Hotel (1866–present), (New) Ship Inn (1831–2011).

WATER STREET, OFF CHURCH STREET, NOW MANCHESTER ROAD (Chapter 2) – Black Swan (1827–91), Griffin Inn (1840–70), Rifleman Inn (1819–1904), Turf Tavern (1818).

WATERSIDE, BOTTOM OF FISHERGATE HILL (Chapter 2) White Horse (1686–1818).

WARD'S END, OFF LANCASTER ROAD, TOWN CENTRE (Chapter 2) – Butchers' Arms (1796–*c.* 1829), later renamed Golden Lion (*c.* 1839–1970s).

WELLFIELD ROAD, OFF MARSH LANE (Chapter 3) – Pedders' Arms (1857–1960s), Ribble View Inn (1851–1960s).

WEST STRAND ROAD, NOW PART OF STRAND ROAD (Chapter 3) – Neptune Hotel (1865–1990s), Old Quay Inn (1869).

WILLIAM STREET, OFF OAK STREET, AVENHAM (Chapter 2) – Fitters' Arms (1856), probably synonymous with The Old House at Home (1851–*c.* 1960), Hearts of Oak (1851–1904), Paradise Tavern (1841–1904).

Acknowledgements

I would like to express my thanks and appreciation to the following organisations and individuals, who have been of assistance to me in the preparation of the book, particularly Barney Smith, site manager of the Preston Digital Archive on Flickr, for his help and encouragement. I am also indebted to the late Jim Holderness, a man I never met. About twelve years ago, his sister gave me his collection of public house images that he had the foresight to create in excess of twenty-five years ago. She gave me them to treat as my own, but I promised her that I would always acknowledge their provenance. Almost all of them can be found on my website, http://pubsinpreston. blogspot.co.uk, and a few will be found in this book.

I would also like to thank Lancashire County Council for allowing me to use the iconic image of the Blue Anchor Inn, which stood where another iconic building, the Harris Museum and Art Gallery, now stands.

Finally, I would like to thank my wife, Rita, for giving me the time and space to complete this endeavour.